Jesus: DEAD or A‿

Jesus: DEAD or ALIVE?

the evidence

by

John B. Dyer

To those who taught me 'The Way'

Contents

Foreword

Even a brief visit to a 'traditional' church building would leave you with the impression that at the heart of the Christian story is the cross (sometimes empty - sometimes occupied). This book does not in any way set out to devalue the cross merely to point out that for the church the resurrection of Jesus is central to its existence, message and mission. Hence the urgency you find here to support a 'reasoned' view that Jesus died and is raised to life on the 'third day'. As with the Apostle Paul the author is in agreement with the statement "And if Christ has not been raised, your faith is futile..." (1 Corinthians 15.17a NIV).

If you are looking for a book that is apologetic in its approach you have found one. It provides a robust 'defence' for belief in the resurrection. Possibly what sets it apart from other 'defences' of the resurrection accounts is that it draws on biblical scholarship and engages in a 'grown up' conversation with those who view the events differently. This is more 'Sherlock Holmes' than 'Inspector Clouseau' in its approach. Although the author sets out on his 'investigation' from a position of belief there is also the sense that he is making some personal discoveries in the biblical accounts of the resurrection. And for that we can be grateful.

The first section of the book addresses the accounts given by the four evangelists. In many ways the book parallels the work of F. Morrison (Who moved the stone? Faber 1958) but for me is more willing to engage with some of the apparent inconsistencies in the four accounts (arguing that they add authenticity to the accounts) alongside some of the more recent insights of biblical scholars. There is no attempt merely to appeal to the emotions but instead to engage the mind and to

11

show in a reasoned way how the pieces of the jigsaw fit together (the reason why the book is written). The author's appeal is to read all four gospels together to see the complete picture emerge and the unified conclusion they draw – Jesus is alive.

There are some good insights to reflect on - the relationship between the resurrection and the ascension being one of them; historical truth and theological insight; the relationship between apocalyptic literature and eschatology; the biblical narrative and the 'secular' evidence from external sources; the significance of non-canonical literature; the role of the Holy Spirit and even a few thoughts on the nature of heaven. Much that will stimulate a desire to go deeper.

The section entitled 'assimilating the evidence' is where I believe the book makes a significant contribution. Focusing on the mission of the early church the emphasis is on the way the resurrection impacted the lives of the early believers as well as provided the core element in their preaching. Drawing on recent scholarship the author is keen to shorten the distance between the oral period and the written one thus adding to its claims for authenticity. It is the resurrection that shapes the church, calls it to mission and inspires it to live as a community.

Seeking to draw us into the narrative and to give that sense that we too are part of the outworking of the resurrection narratives, the author charts briefly the call of the church to continue to draw its 'raison d'etre' from the events that the followers of Jesus first bore witness to. The challenge is to a personal experience of the risen Christ where Jesus becomes our 'Lord' and our response leads to worship. In the author's words "As for the church, yesterday and today, it exists solely in consequence of the Resurrection."

Stephen Cave, Broadstairs.

Preface

For many years I have studied the resurrection stories in the Gospels and have been held captive by the extraordinary claim that after being pronounced dead by the Roman authorities and buried in a Jewish grave, Jesus rose again. In a perhaps less than critical way, I accepted the facts as given and also allowed for the discrepancies between one account and the other, when comparing and contrasting the different versions of this unique event in history.

Even so, none of us are born believers in these things; none of us are convinced Christians as a default setting at birth. Jesus, himself, made this point very clearly in a conversation with a secret follower named Nicodemus (who was a member of the Jewish ruling council, the Sanhedrin). It is from this conversation between Jesus and Nicodemus that we get the notion of being 'born again' to a life of faith and witness (John 3.3). Usually we become Christians through a persuasive sermon or from taking part in a series of Bible studies. This experience of new life is brought about by the inward working of the Holy Spirit, stirring our hearts and minds (like the wind blowing through the trees), as we hear and read about the things that Jesus taught and did, and most especially of what happened on that incredible resurrection morning 2000 years ago.

This book is written for those who are willing to interact and engage with that familiar story. It is also intended for those curious to make connections with the cultural and psychological nuances within the story as well as the arguments for and against the plausibility of the main

13

plot. Taking the narratives as they stand, is it doubtful, possible or strangely probable that the story is based on events that really happened? The sceptic would say that we simply cannot know what the truth of the matter really is, because truth is unknowable. This is, however, an affirmation that truth exists, even if it is unknowable. Our pluralistic and relativistic society would say that truth is what each individual wants or considers it to be. So, where there are a variety of opinions, no particular one is right or wrong, and there is no absolute truth by which all others are measured to determine their degree of accuracy. From this perspective, there are many truths, which again is an affirmation that truth does exist, albeit as a multi-faceted concept. In our present investigation, we shall take a closer look at the resurrection story and the different groups of people involved, from the inner band of disciples to the antagonistic priestly aristocracy with their respective interests, expectations and concerns regarding Jesus of Nazareth. A number of questions are raised during the course of our investigation: Do the different biblical accounts stand up to closer scrutiny? Is Jesus Christ, or any of his followers mentioned anywhere outside the Bible? If he did rise from the dead, what kind of body did he have after the Resurrection? Was it different in any way from the body that was laid in the tomb? If so, in what sense was it perceived to be different? Can the resurrection of Jesus make a difference to us? And if so, 'how'? My objective is to respond to these questions by focusing closely on the evidence at our disposal.

I am grateful to friends who have read the text of this book prior to publication and have made invaluable

Preface

observations and comments. Though written from the perspective of one who is a follower of Jesus, through the witness of other followers who showed me the way, the purpose in writing this book is not to win over the doubters or detractors by powers of persuasion. It is written for the purpose of allowing the story to speak for itself with the help of *insights* that are sometimes, if not often, missed by the casual reader, and even the habitual reader, who is already familiar with the story. I have found that there are hidden details within and behind the text, that are not always easily seen to be there, but nonetheless exist. It is like seeing the outline of a human face or other form within a series of differently coloured dots. Of course, if one happens to be colour blind, it might become quite difficult or even impossible to make out any figure at all within the multi-coloured dots. This analogy might have its limitations, but the point is that there is an image *within* the array of dots and colours. It is the same with the story of Easter. It depends on how we look at it and how our brain responds to what we are looking at. But like Nicodemus, for us too, with a little prompting and inquisitive intuition, the unimaginable might possibly turn out to be true: *"For no-one could perform the miraculous signs you are doing if God were not with him."* (John 3.2).

Birchington, Kent. September, 2019.

Prologue

A wise and scholarly pastor once encouraged his flock on the Sunday after Easter to go on thinking about this most important of days in human history. He invited us to focus not only on the event of the Resurrection itself, but also the appearances of Jesus during the days and weeks following that event. In this short book, we shall adhere to his advice as we seek to come to terms with all the ramifications of that event for our own lives and for our understanding of what happened during the forty days between the resurrection of Jesus and his ascension to heaven. Some things in this book will be familiar to many, but others might surprise us as we look more closely at the sequence of events recorded in the Gospels, the Acts of the Apostles, the writings of the Apostle Paul, and take a brief glimpse into the opening chapter of the Book of Revelation.

The resurrection appearances of Jesus took place during forty days, between Easter Sunday and the Ascension, in two distinct geographical locations. First in Jerusalem, then in Galilee, then again in Jerusalem. The *angel* at the tomb (Matthew 28) told the women (the first to arrive there) that Jesus would go ahead of the disciples into Galilee. Then *Jesus*, himself, meets the women on their return to the city and gives them the same message. But before he is seen in *Galilee*, he is seen by the inner circle of disciples in *Jerusalem* (although the evidence is not entirely consistent in this respect) and by two others on their journey from *Jerusalem to Emmaus*. We would assume that the disciples were still in Jerusalem in the immediate days after the Resurrection, and that it was there

17

that Jesus first met them. On balance, the weight of evidence found in the earliest traditions would lend support to this.

For us today, the significance of Jesus' appearances in Galilee is that it is a pointer to his being found *in the places where we live and work.* Galilee was the scene of the disciples' daily lives, many of whom were fishermen. Seven of the eleven were in their boat fishing when Jesus appeared to them on a beach along the Sea of Galilee. According to John, this was the *third* time he appeared to the disciples after his resurrection. Though Jerusalem was the centre of Jewish religious and political life, it was not where the disciples spent most of their time. The significance of these passages is that they indicate that Jesus takes the initiative by coming to us, as he did at his incarnation in Bethlehem. So, where can we spend time with him and walk in his presence, *today*? Indeed, we are not only dealing with history as 'past event', but also with the present 'here and now' and also a future concerned with what is 'yet to be'. This point is made by George R. Beasley-Murray in his invitation to take a closer look at the Resurrection: 'towards it, ages moved, from it they advance.' *(The Resurrection of Jesus Christ)*. In a similar way, the distinguished Lutheran theologian, Oscar Cullmann, places the redemptive act of the cross and resurrection exactly and strategically at the 'mid-point' of history (*Christ and Time,* Part II). The cross and resurrection reach backwards and forwards in time, encompassing all of history; and, therefore, have to do with *all of us.*

Prologue

In this short book, we shall look at the evidence presented in the Gospels, as well as that from historical sources outside the Bible (extra-biblical material). We shall also hear, and respond to, the different theories put forward against the notion that the Resurrection took place at all. That is, that it happened as a historical event on a given date outside the ancient walls of a Middle Eastern city. The kaleidoscope of different facets will overlap as we contemplate them and return to them for further insights. These will elucidate and interpret the information we are attempting to process through reflection and investigation. Ultimately, it is the Bible that interprets the Bible, and it is to the eyewitness themselves that we shall look as we progress in our appreciation and understanding of their testimony. We may be surprised to find that the accounts given in the four Gospels have already anticipated the *objections* to the idea of a factual and historical resurrection. Are these challenges to the Resurrection genuine attempts to establish the truth, straws in the wind, or a desperate attempt to bury the truth? We shall see. The main theories advanced in opposition to the Resurrection are as follows: firstly, that the body of Jesus was removed by his disciples and placed in another tomb; secondly, that Jesus did not really die, and had resuscitated in the cool of the tomb; thirdly, that the women who went to the tomb on the third day, had mistaken it for another; fourthly, that the disciples only imagined they had seen Jesus alive after he was buried in the tomb, and were having hallucinations. We will not detail the responses that we find in the Gospels themselves, or our own assessment for the moment, but will respond to each theory as the situation arises during the course of this book.

At the close of the Fourth Gospel, the writer states that Jesus performed many other miraculous signs not recorded by him. We may presume that these are written down in the *synoptic gospels* or simply remembered by way of the different *oral traditions*, which were handed down by the first-hand witnesses and those close to them. We do know that the whole story is bigger than even that which we have in our New Testament. Everyone who knew Jesus had a story to tell. And these stories are told with a clear purpose in mind; to show that Jesus is the Christ, the Son of God, who defeated death and left the tomb behind. The different stories represent different recollections and priorities concerning the original events. If there was only one account, we would be the poorer for not knowing as much as we do know. On the other hand, multiple versions of the same story, though allowing us to see the events from many different angles and from the different memory stores of those who were there at the time, also include variations and apparent contradictions in the way the story has been remembered. To use an analogy, if different members of the same family were to send postcards from holiday, the news shared would not be identical. Each writer would have their priorities regarding what was important to share about their holiday and they would organise these priorities accordingly. For one the sun shone every day, for another it occasionally rained. However, we may assume that there would be agreement in relation to the country or people they were visiting. The story of the Resurrection contains many facets and draws on the memory and recollections of different people, from different occupations, backgrounds and temperaments. There is, nonetheless, a compelling consistency regarding the main plot. In the world of politics and diplomacy, if there are things that unite us and others that divide us, we try to find the common ground upon which we are all agreed. That is also true of storytelling. After all, the central message of the story takes pre-eminence over differences in the detail.

This brings us to the reliability of the witnesses themselves. For example, the *testimony of women* was not taken seriously in the first century Jewish world; and, after all, it was a group of women followers of Jesus who were the first to witness this unprecedented event in history. Herein lies a twist in the *tale*. If the story is meant to be trusted, then why include witnesses whose testimony might discredit it or cast doubt on it? The answer to this conundrum may lie in the possibility that the events took place (with variations) exactly as they are told.

How important was historical truth to the writers of the four Gospels? The science of recording historical events was different in the ancient world. The *reason* for telling the story was often more important than historical accuracy. This comes through in the four Gospels. For example, the target audience (revealing the purpose for writing) can be clearly defined in each case by the way the story is told: Mark for the Roman world, Matthew for the Jewish and Luke for the Greek speaking world. John, on the other hand, is reckoned to have written to counter false Gnostic and docetic interpretations of the person of Jesus (which denied his true humanity), thus John's particular emphasis on the real physical body of Jesus from his birth to his resurrection. But the overall purpose in all four Gospels is to glorify Jesus. This has caused some experts in biblical criticism to say that mythological and supernatural elements were added, therefore casting doubt on the historical reliability of the story as a whole. Having said that, the fact of specific motivation does not necessarily exclude the basis in truth and objectivity of the story told. We shall now move on to the story and the storytellers, as we seek to unravel truth from speculation on both sides of the argument.

PART ONE

Approaching the Evidence

Chapter One

In the Synoptic Gospels

According to Mark

Outline

To start us on our way, we shall look at the story as handed down to us by the first-hand witnesses. We begin with the Gospel of Mark, because it is the original account, the first of the four Gospels to be written. It is the nearest to the time the events took place and within the lifetime of many of the generation that was present in Jerusalem the day that Jesus of Nazareth was crucified. Those of this group who were still alive would have been able to contest the unfolding story, if they had reason to do so. What is more, the author of this Gospel is John Mark, the son of Mary, in whose house in Jerusalem Jesus celebrated the Last Supper with his disciples and where those same disciples gathered together behind closed doors on Good Friday. It was here that Jesus appeared to his disciples on Easter Sunday evening and the Sunday following his resurrection. In this case, John Mark would have been close to the events that took place in Jerusalem during those days.

Jesus: Dead or Alive?

And this is how he records those events: Early on the first day of the week, just after sunrise, Mary Magdalene, Mary the mother of James, and Salome went to the tomb with spices in order to anoint the body of Jesus. They were concerned as to who would remove the stone. On arriving at the tomb, they discovered that the stone had already been rolled away, and upon entering saw a young man dressed in white sitting on the right side of the slab where the body of Jesus had been laid. They expressed alarm at the sight.

The young man told them not to be alarmed. He knew that they were looking for Jesus the Nazarene who had been crucified. He then informed the women that Jesus was no longer in the tomb, but had risen from the dead. He invited the women to see the place where the body of Jesus had been laid. The young man then told the women to go and tell the disciples and Peter that Jesus was going ahead of them into Galilee, where they would see him. If we rewind to Mark's description of the scene in the Garden of Gethsemane, we will see that Jesus had said exactly this to his disciples (on their way to the Mount of Olives, Mark 14.28). The reference to Galilee by the young man in the tomb is therefore consistent with what Jesus is reported to have said and also provides an argument for the integrity (trustworthiness) of the central message. The women then fled from the tomb and said nothing to anyone because they were afraid.

In the Synoptic Gospels

Commentary

There is a rather abrupt ending to the original version of the Gospel of Mark. It is generally accepted that the original longer ending has been lost and that the ending which we have today was added later. It is unlikely that Mark would have stopped writing at the point where the women fled from the tomb in fear and bewilderment. Nonetheless, Frank Morison, in his book *Who Moved the Stone?* argues that this is a most important fragment of literature for the purpose of understanding this extraordinary event and also the accounts given by Matthew and Luke. That aside, the appearance of an angel (Matthew) and two angels (Luke) are considered by Morison to have been added later by the first century church.

Morison gives considerable weight to the Gospel of the Hebrews (a Jewish Christian form of the canonical Gospel of Matthew), which refers to 'the servant of the priest' to whom Jesus is said to have given the folded head cloth. In this the case, with such a handy witness, the priests would have known exactly what happened and how the stone was rolled away. According to Matthew, they elaborated a coverup story with the guards that the disciples had stolen the body of Jesus. This would naturally lend weight to the fact that Jesus had left the tomb in circumstances that nobody knew or that the priests preferred to keep secret. Nevertheless, the 'servant of the priest theory' is not without its own problems. The Gospel of the Hebrews (the bearer of this part of the story) gradually fell out of use and was not accorded the authority of the canonical gospels, when these were officially recognised in the fourth century. Having said that, this Gospel *is* known to have been relied upon by the Church Fathers in the East, including Clement of Alexandria and Origen, as source material for their own literary output. In the West, Jerome also quoted extensively from the text of this Hebrew Gospel. Taking this on board, we may reasonably assume that it was, at least for a time, considered to be a *significant* document.

Returning to the abrupt ending to the Gospel of Mark, Morison argues from the 'Messianic Secret' (regarding the silence imposed by Jesus on certain individuals, with the purpose of averting public acknowledgement that he was the Messiah). Morison uses this to explain the silence of the women in Mark's Gospel, "They said nothing to anyone." The instruction to maintain silence is a characteristic of this gospel.

The singular importance of Mark's account of events rests in the fact that he was a resident of Jerusalem when these things took place. William Neil in *The Life and Teaching of Jesus*, pp. 40-42, draws attention to the fact that tradition dating back to Papias, is unanimous in saying that the author of this Gospel was John Mark, a contemporary of John the Elder (who we shall meet later in this book). In fact, the disciples of Jesus often met in John Mark's house after the Resurrection (Acts 12.12). It is also possible that Jesus held the Last Supper in the upper room of this house, and quite likely that John Mark is the young man who fled naked from the Garden of Gethsemane, when Jesus was arrested there; this is all the more plausible if Jesus went from the house of John Mark directly to the Garden late that evening, and John Mark had followed him there. In the context of the story, this particular detail concerning the young man would hardly have been mentioned unless it were true (Mark 14.51-52). The fact that Mark devotes more than a third of his Gospel to this single week of a three-year ministry should not surprise us, considering how close he was to the events of that unparalleled week in history. More than many, he could say: "I was *there* when they crucified my Lord." He could also say, "I was *there* when he rose up from the grave." Even if he was not an *eyewitness* to the crucifixion and Resurrection, at the very least he was in the vicinity when these events took place and would have been among the first to hear of those events. It is widely agreed that Mark wrote his Gospel in Rome, about three decades after the events he describes and that his material was obtained from Peter. It is to be expected that he would write mostly about the things he knew best; the things about which he had heard or gleaned from information to which he had unique access in Jerusalem, those three decades earlier. For this reason, he would have been a substantial authority on these matters and well placed to write about them.

I have not used the longer ending of Mark for establishing the facts concerning the Easter story. Without the lost ending, there is no evidence in Mark's Gospel of the resurrection appearances of Jesus. But we do have evidence of the empty tomb and reason to believe that Jesus *was* raised from the dead. The manner of his appearing is not covered by Mark, though it may have been in the so-called 'Lost Ending'. We simply do not know. The ending, as we have it, is generally believed by scholars to be the work of another writer. The themes of this ending follow the traditions of Matthew and Luke, and these two may well have been relied upon to write the ending of Mark's Gospel. There is, for example, a mention of the disbelief of the disciples on hearing the report of the women and also a reference to Jesus appearing to two disciples in the countryside. The Ascension is also included, as in Luke. Further, there is an appearance with a commissioning of the disciples, as in Matthew, but this would seem to have happened in Jerusalem, rather than Galilee, though no specific location is mentioned. So how do the pieces of the puzzle fit together? The answer to this question is the reason for writing this book.

In the Synoptic Gospels

According to Matthew

Outline

We shall now relate the sequence of events as described by Matthew, the personalities involved and their reactions, as they sought to assimilate the startling news that the body of Jesus was no longer in the tomb.

On the first day of the week, at daybreak, Mary Magdalene and the other Mary went to the tomb. There was an earthquake, and an angel, whose appearance was like lightning. He was clothed in white, he rolled back the stone and sat on it. The guards were terrified at the sight and were unable to move, so great was their fear. The angel told the women that Jesus had risen from the dead and was no longer there. The angel invited the women to observe the place where the body of Jesus had been laid. He then told them to inform the other disciples that Jesus had gone ahead of them into Galilee, where they would see him. The women left the tomb afraid, but filled with joy, and ran to tell the disciples. Jesus then appeared to the women and greeted them. They clasped his feet and worshipped him. He told them not to be afraid and repeated the command of the angel for them to go to Galilee with the disciples, where he would meet them. The soldiers were bribed by the chief priests and elders to say that the disciples had stolen the body of Jesus while they (the soldiers) were asleep. The disciples went to Galilee to the mountain where Jesus had instructed them to go. There they saw him and worshipped him, though some doubted. Then Jesus commissioned them to go into all the world and make disciples with the promise that he would always be with them.

Commentary

As in all four Gospels, it was the women who went first to the tomb as dawn was breaking over Jerusalem. There are differences as to who exactly went and whether they took spices in order to anoint the body of Jesus. There is, however, no divergence in the story as to what they found when they arrived there. The stone had been removed. It is unclear whether there was one angel, two angels or a young man, who may also have been an angel, that greeted the women with the news that Jesus was no longer there. They are all agreed that the body of Jesus had not been *removed* from the tomb. There is no apparent indication from what they say that this is what had happened. What they *do* say, emphatically and in unison, is that Jesus was not there, because he was no longer dead, but had *risen*.

Moving further into the story, it is quite probable that the 'more than five hundred disciples' who saw the risen Lord (to whom Paul refers in 1 Corinthians 15.6), were those who later gathered with the eleven at the mountain in Galilee (Matthew 28.16-17). Dr Elizabeth Mitchell, in an article entitled 'The Sequence of Christ's Post-Resurrection Appearances' makes the point that "by this time word of Christ's promised appearance would have spread among his many followers and given them time to arrive." It was likely that those who still doubted were not of the eleven, but this wider circle of followers who had not yet seen Jesus after his resurrection.

In the Synoptic Gospels

There is one further observation that I should like to make, following on from Matthew's account of the Resurrection: the story pertaining to the guards on duty at the tomb would hold no water, since they could not possibly have known *how* the body of Jesus was removed from the tomb, or *by whom*, if they were *asleep* at the time. The priests, on the other hand, would have known more than they were prepared to admit. Otherwise they would *not* have offered to protect the soldiers from the Roman authorities, but rather would have demanded that they find the body. This is basically the conclusion to Frank Morrison's detailed investigation in his book, *Who Moved the Stone*? Further, we are given to understand that the request for the Roman authorities to place a guard at the tomb was turned down by Pilate. In that case the soldiers would have been from the Temple Guard, as Morison suspects, and so Pilate would have had little interest or involvement in the matter, to match his 'neutrality' from the start.

But there remains one other unanswered question concerning the guard placed at the tomb. The soldiers must have known what happened, even if no one else did. Of that we can be sure. What we *do* know is that the story put around by the priests in collaboration with the guard was a fabrication. To obtain the participation of the guard in such a story, the priests had paid them a handsome bribe. We do not know what the soldiers said to the priests, but whatever it was, it would have been of great concern to the religious hierarchy. So, what was it that happened that night?

Morison, himself a sceptic for many years, writes at the close of his book, the following haunting words:

33

Jesus: Dead or Alive?

> I have an impression... that as dawn
> approached in that quiet garden,
> something happened which caused one
> of the watchers hurriedly to awaken his
> companions and to proceed to a closer
> inspection of the tomb. It may have
> been only the stirring of the trees, or the
> clanging of a gate in the night breeze. It
> may have been something more definite
> and disquieting, such as that which later
> shook and utterly humbled the proud
> and relentless spirit of St. Paul. (p. 192).

Apart from this story of the guard, Matthew uses
only the Galilean tradition concerning the resurrection
appearances of Jesus. This connects with the words spoken
to the women by the angel and Jesus, himself, that he
would go before them into *Galilee*. Matthew differs in this
respect from Luke and John who both report that Jesus
appeared to the disciples in Jerusalem. The direct link
between the empty tomb and resurrection appearance in
Galilee (in Matthew's Gospel) lends support to the unlikely
idea that the disciples returned immediately to Galilee.
Further appearances, (not in Matthew), are detailed by
Mark, Luke and John as follows: the material appended to
Mark's Gospel refers to two disciples meeting with Jesus
as they walked in the country, (reminiscent of the Lucan
account of the two disciples on their homeward journey to
Emmaus) and that they returned (presumably to Jerusalem)
and reported this to the disciples gathered there. Their

report, however, was received with disbelief, which is contrary to how Luke describes that same moment, when the disciples in Jerusalem confirmed the report, saying that the Lord had appeared to Peter. John's reference to a Galilean appearance is found in the last chapter of his Gospel, which is generally understood to be a *later* addition, and possibly for the purpose of including the reinstatement of Peter as a pastor and leader of the church. As is becoming slowly evident, it is of the essence to read the *four* Gospels *together*, in order to see the bigger picture.

Jesus: Dead or Alive?

According to Luke

Outline

In Luke's account, the details are slightly different, but the overall message is the same. The women went to the tomb very early with spices. When they arrived, the stone had already been rolled away and the body of Jesus was no longer there. Suddenly two men in clothes that gleamed like lightning stood before them. The frightened women bowed down before the angelic figures. The two men asked the women why they were seeking the living among the dead. They then reminded the women of what Jesus had said; that he must be delivered into the hands of sinful men, be crucified and on the third day be raised again. Mary Magdalene, Mary the mother of James and also Joanna were named as being the women present at the tomb. When the women told the disciples about this, they did not believe their report and assumed they were speaking nonsense. Peter, however, ran to the tomb and saw the linen strips lying by themselves. He could not understand what had happened.

That evening, two other disciples were returning home from Jerusalem (now this story is unique to Luke). Their journey took them along the road to Emmaus, a village some seven miles northwest of Jerusalem. They were talking about the things that had happened in Jerusalem, when Jesus came up to them and walked along with them; but the two disciples did not recognise him. When Jesus asked what it was they were talking about, they, downcast in spirit, paused, surprised that this 'stranger' did not know about the events of the previous few days. Jesus then asked them, 'What things?' The story then unfolded of how Jesus of Nazareth had been crucified, a prophet powerful in word and deed, in whom they had hoped Israel would be redeemed. They then related to Jesus the stories about the empty tomb and the angels who said he was alive. With that, Jesus admonished them and began to explain from Scripture how these things were foretold by Moses and the prophets, and how God's Messiah, the Christ, would rise again. As it was late, the two disciples invited Jesus into their home. He accepted their invitation to rest before continuing his journey and, assuming the role of the host, he gave thanks and broke the bread. As he did so, they recognised that it was Jesus with whom they had been speaking along the way, and that it was Jesus who was reclining before them as they participated in the evening meal. With that he disappeared from their sight, and they were left discussing how their hearts had been stirred as he spoke to them and opened the Scriptures to them on the journey home.

Immediately, they returned to Jerusalem with the news, and already (so they were told by the disciples gathered there), Jesus had appeared to Peter. In that same moment, Jesus stood among them and greeted them with the words: 'Peace be with you.' At this point in Luke's account, we note his characteristic emphasis on the humanity of Jesus and that he still had a physical body. He could eat food and be touched in the same way as anyone else. Nevertheless, Jesus' resurrection body was different from the body he had before. Though discernibly different, it was tangible and could be touched. Jesus then introduces

the disciples to the next stage of events. They would
receive power to be his witnesses in the world, beginning
in Jerusalem. But before this could happen, he had to return
to the Father as he said he would. He then leads them out
to the vicinity of Bethany, about one-and-a-half miles east
from Jerusalem. There he bids them a final farewell and is
received into heaven. The disciples worshipped him and
returned to Jerusalem with great joy in their hearts, praising
God in the temple.

Commentary

The effect of this hugely significant event on the disciples
was obvious, though there was not an immediate break
with the traditions of temple worship. Whilst they broke
bread in one another's homes (Acts 2.46), it is not clear
from the book of Acts, whether this happened once a week,
on the first day of the week, or more frequently. But it is
evident that they remained very Jewish in their outlook and
the new church was essentially *a movement within
Judaism*. The full meaning of the new faith needed to be
revealed gradually, as time passed, for which we have
further evidence in Luke's second volume, the Book of
Acts.

There are two further aspects of the story to which
our attention should be drawn as we compare Luke's
account with the other Gospel accounts of the
Resurrection: firstly, Luke records that Peter ran to the
tomb on hearing the report from the women that it was
empty. In the account given in the Fourth Gospel, both
Peter and John ran to the tomb. We are also treated to the

added detail that John arrived first (and being the younger of the two, this would be quite natural). It is almost as if the writer were saying that the disciple who arrived first was in fact *him*. Of course, this technique is not unknown in the world of art and film. For example, Rembrandt appears in the shadows, among the characters in his painting 'The Return of the Prodigal Son'. This is not explicit, but the similarity is obvious. The film director, Alfred Hitchcock, does the same by appearing momentarily in one of the scenes from each of his films. The Gospel writer, John Mark, does something similar when he introduces a cameo of a young man who followed Jesus into the Garden of Gethsemane; the inference that it is John Mark, himself, is difficult to avoid (Mark 14.51). If the apostle, or someone close to him, wrote the Fourth Gospel, we could here be privy to historical detail, absent from the other Gospel accounts. Irenaeus, a disciple of Polycarp (who was a direct disciple of the apostle John) seems to accept that John either wrote the Gospel that bears his name or was at least involved in writing it (see 'Irenaeus against Heresies, 1.8.5'). Of course, John would have had special interest in including himself in the Gospel narrative, if he were an eyewitness to the things he is describing as, for example, in the references to 'the disciple whom Jesus loved' a familiar turn of phrase in the Fourth Gospel. However, Luke would not have the same degree of interest in this, and would have researched his account of events from third-party sources. The apparent discrepancies are, therefore, tolerable and, in any case, do not detract from the central message of the gospel. It is even likely that John's account is historically more accurate than Luke's at this point.

Secondly, there is an immediate connection in Luke's account between the appearances of Jesus in Jerusalem and his ascension at Bethany. There is no reference to the Galilean appearances, neither is there an obvious period of forty days between the Resurrection and the Ascension. Significantly, Luke does mention the forty days in the opening chapter of his second book, the Acts of the Apostles, which would allow time for the appearances in Galilee. If one takes time to consider the bigger picture, as well as the discrepancy in the detail, the Lucan and Johannine approaches both draw exactly the same conclusion. The tomb was empty, and Jesus was seen to be alive from the third day onwards.

Luke, as we have already observed, focuses on the human side of things, and this comes through with no greater force than after the Resurrection. There were two angelic figures *like men* at the tomb to meet the women. They gently remind the women of the words of Jesus before his crucifixion. There is compassion in their words, and the women are able to remember those words of Jesus. That evening, on the road to Emmaus, Jesus takes time to explain to two disciples returning home from Jerusalem that the cross was a necessary part of God's plan as foretold in all the Scriptures. He opens their eyes to these things. Later, when he appears to the disciples in Jerusalem, he does so in full *bodily* form: "Why are you troubled, and why do doubts rise in your minds? Look at my hands and my feet. Touch me and see; a ghost does not have flesh and bones, as you see I have." (Luke 24.38-39). Then he asked for something to eat, in order to prove his point. In all three Lucan appearances there is a call to the human senses: hearing, sight and touch, to grasp the fact that the Resurrection was real, recognisable and tangible.

A helpful survey by Professor F. F. Bruce in his, *The New Testament Documents,* indicates that Luke obtained his material from sources close to the events he records, namely: John Mark and Paul, with whom he spent time in Rome (Acts 28.11-16; 2 Timothy 4.11); Philip whom he knew in Caesarea (Acts 21.8f) and from whom he was able to obtain much of the material used for the third Gospel and Acts. He is also known to have had contact with James the brother of Jesus: "When we arrived at Jerusalem, the brothers received us warmly. The next day Paul and the rest of us went to see James, and all the elders were present." (Acts 21.17-18). Therefore, there was no lack of primary sources, and of those close to the apostles, from which he could research the material for his narratives.

Chapter Two

In the Gospel of John

Outline

John's approach brings to light an interesting point about the relationship of the Resurrection to the Ascension, and how and when the second phase of this two-fold event took place. He also introduces a story not found in the other Gospels concerning the appearance of Jesus on the shore of the Sea of Galilee, which he records as the third appearance of Jesus to the disciples. Beset by apparent frustration, Peter decides to go fishing and is joined by some of the other disciples. After a wasted night during which they caught nothing, Jesus appears on the beach and instructs them to cast their nets to the other side of the boat. The catch is truly spectacular, there being so many fish, they could hardly drag their nets to the shore. Jesus has already prepared breakfast on the beach. John is the first of the group to recognise that it is Jesus, and Peter, true to character, puts on his tunic and is soon in the water and swimming to the shore. Winding back the clock to Easter Sunday, John's account runs like this: on the first day of the week, while it was still dark, Mary Magdalene went out from Jerusalem to the garden tomb. To her surprise, the heavy stone sealing the entrance to the tomb had been removed and the body of Jesus was no longer there. She returned at once to the city to tell Peter and John of her discovery: "They have taken the Lord out of the tomb, and we don't know where they have put him!" (John 20.2). Peter and John then came running to the tomb. John arrived first and stood at the entrance. He looked in and saw the grave clothes, but did not enter the tomb. Peter arrived after John and, true to character, immediately entered the tomb. He saw the linen strips and the burial cloth, which was folded up separately. Then John entered the tomb, and when he saw he believed.

The two disciples returned to their homes, but Mary Magdalene remained at the tomb. She looked into the tomb and saw two angels sitting where the body of Jesus had been laid, one at the head and the other at the foot. She then turned and saw Jesus standing there, though she did not recognise him. He asked why she was crying and who she was looking for? Thinking he was the gardener she asked if he had removed the body of Jesus. At that moment, Jesus called Mary by her name and she recognised his voice and knew, immediately, that the one she had thought to be the gardener was, in fact, Jesus. He resisted her attempt to cling to him, saying that he had not yet returned to the Father and that she should go and tell the other disciples that he was returning to the Father. She immediately returned to the disciples and told them that she had seen Jesus and also the things he had spoken to her.

That evening, Jesus came to the disciples. They were in hiding behind locked doors 'for fear of the Jews.' He greeted them with the words 'Peace be with you' and showed them his hands and his side. They were overjoyed to see him. Again, he greeted them with the words, 'Peace be with you' and breathed on them his Spirit. He then commissioned them to go into the world in his name.

The following Sunday, Thomas, who was absent when he appeared to his disciples the week before, was now present. They told him that they had seen Jesus, but he said he would not believe them unless he saw for himself. Jesus then appeared to the disciples again, though the doors were locked. Once more he greeted them with the words, 'Peace be with you.' He then invited Thomas to see his wounds and place his hand into his side. With this visual confirmation of the Resurrection, Thomas confessed Jesus as Lord and God. Jesus then pronounced blessing on those who believed on him without the benefit of visible proof (John 20.29).

After that Jesus appeared to his disciples one morning on the shore of Galilee. John was the first to recognise him, but Peter was first to reach Jesus, having jumped into the water and swimming to the shore. Jesus had a fire going and fish on the coals, also some bread. The disciples also contributed with some of the fish they had caught. Jesus then recommissioned Peter with pastoral charge over the flock of God. John tells us that this was the third time Jesus had appeared to his disciples after the Resurrection. Although this last section of John's Gospel was added at a later date, the language style and vocabulary would suggest it was by the same author as the preceding chapters. Moreover, the details given of the disciples who were present on this occasion, reveal characteristic behavioural traits, thus lending authenticity to this third appearance of Jesus to his disciples as a group.

Jesus: Dead or Alive?

In adding this final chapter, John is anxious to correct a misunderstanding concerning 'the disciple whom Jesus loved' (21.20). The internal evidence is that the writer prioritised the accuracy of the record of the life and teaching of Jesus that he was leaving for his and future generations: "This is the disciple who testifies to these things and who wrote them down. *We know that his testimony is true*" (21.24). From this, it would appear that there were witnesses to the writing of this Gospel, and witnesses who were prepared to vouch for its authenticity.

Commentary

George Beasley-Murray, in his book *The Resurrection of Jesus Christ,* based on a series of radio broadcasts, makes the following insightful comment:

> In the ancient book of Leviticus, it is commanded that a first sheaf of the barley harvest be brought into the temple on the day after Passover to sanctify the whole harvest. Now Good Friday, when Jesus died, was the day before Passover that year; Passover was the second day; the day after Passover was the third day, Easter Sunday. On the day when the first sheaf to consecrate the harvest was brought to God, Jesus rose, the first of the harvest of resurrection of the race.

In the Gospel of John

Though the facts apply to all four gospel records, John brings out yet another amazing insight when he places the time of Christ's death at the very moment the lambs would have been killed in preparation for the Passover meal. The gospels are records of events that actually happened in history, but behind the events there is also a deep theological significance to be grasped. This is 'the message of the gospel', which the writer wants us to receive.

The theory has been put forward from time to time that Jesus may not have died on the cross, but merely swooned and that after he was taken down from the cross and buried in the tomb he revived. This theory is advanced in order to give a rational answer to an imponderable question. However, we can prove from the evidence we have, that he had in fact died, which fact was confirmed by the Roman soldiers at the cross: "But when they came to Jesus and saw that he was already dead, they did not break his legs. Instead, one of the soldiers pierced Jesus' side with a spear, bringing a sudden flow of blood and water." (John 19.33-34). Now the writer pays special attention to this by claiming that it is based on the testimony of an eye-witness, and whose testimony is trustworthy (19.35).

It is important also that we recall the fact that when the soldier pierced Jesus' side, both blood and water came out. The blood and water were separate. When the heart stops, the blood in it would coagulate forming clots and serum. The spear, when thrust into Jesus' side, released clots of blood and serum, because Jesus really died. Though serum is a clear yellowish fluid, in the available light, it would have looked no different from water. Do we

47

need to advance further arguments against the theory that Jesus revived in the tomb? Though John puts the sequence in the order 'blood and water', when, in fact, water would have poured out first, the blood was more dramatic as well as greater in quantity. The fact is both blood *and* water gushed out from Jesus' side; so we will not split hairs. As inconvenient as it may be for this particular theory and those who advance it, Jesus did, in fact, *die* on the cross. The Roman soldiers were well experienced in performing executions and this final act of brutality was engineered to ensure that death had definitely occurred.

John also informs us that the body of Jesus was anointed with spices on the day of his burial and that these were provided by Nicodemus, the secret disciple who came to Jesus by night (John 3.1ff). According to John the Jewish burial rites were performed by Nicodemus and Joseph of Arimathea, whose tomb it was. Unlike the synoptic gospels, John gives the impression that on Easter Sunday morning, Mary Magdalene went to the tomb alone. But if we look at the detail in John's account, we discover something very interesting in this respect, which brings him into agreement with the synoptic traditions. However, I shall return to this later. Matthew says that Mary Magdalene and the other Mary went to look at the tomb, with no mention of their taking spices to anoint the body of Jesus. Taken together, these divergencies are simply different ways of recalling the same historical event. There is no apparent or inherent contradiction in the accounts themselves.

In his teaching concerning the incarnation (which is intrinsically bound up with the cross in every sense), John declared "we have seen his *glory*" (my italics). I well remember George Beasley-Murray in one of his New Testament lectures at Spurgeon's College saying that Jesus' glory was 'veiled' (this is particularly true between the resurrection and ascension). This was for the very reason that we could not possibly bear to look upon his *full* glory with mortal eyes. This 'veiled' glory can be seen in the ascension process between resurrection morning and the day of his last appearance to his disciples at Bethany. Though it is Luke who describes this event, it is John who gives us the clear impression that the ascension was a process, accomplished in stages: "his being lifted up on the cross is in fact regarded as the beginning of the ascension" (R.V.G. Tasker, *The Gospel According to St. John*). After the Resurrection, the body of Jesus had undoubtedly changed. Though he was still clearly recognisable from his speech and physical presence, he was at the same time *different*.

The disciples returning to Emmaus had difficulty in recognising Jesus to begin with. Likewise, Mary Magdalene mistook him for the gardener in the first light of resurrection morning. His glory was now being revealed as never before. Subsequent to the forty days and his last appearance to the disciples, the post-ascension appearances were unparalleled in beauty and intensity. Stephen, before his demise, saw the glory of God, and Jesus standing at the right hand of God (Acts 7.55-56). His declaration to this effect was the final straw for his opponents who "rushed at him, dragged him out of the city and began to stone him." (7.57-58). The reaction that Stephen drew from *the Jewish authorities* was in marked contrast to that of *the crowd* on hearing Peter's sermon on the Day of Pentecost. Then it was one of *repentance towards God* for what they had done to Jesus. By contrast, the religious authorities responded with *anger and rage towards Stephen*. Saul, who was among those who consented to the stoning of Stephen, later saw Jesus, for himself, as a light from heaven, so bright that he was blinded for three days (Acts 9.3-9). His description of this encounter confirms, one might say, Stephen's declaration concerning Jesus' position of universal authority and power over all things.

John is the third of our biblical witnesses to have seen the risen Christ after his ascension, "shining like the noon-day sun in all its brilliance." (Revelation 1.16). This Jesus was the same *person* as the 'flesh and bones' Jesus we meet in Luke's Gospel (24.39). In his own words, the risen Christ was *not a phantom*, any more than the Jesus who walked on the Sea of Galilee, to the astonishment of his disciples. The glorification of Jesus was progressive. It happened in stages, beginning with his death on the cross. It is to the cross that Jesus alludes in his request to God: "Father, the time has come. Glorify your Son, that your Son may glorify you" (John 17.1). His glorification (at least to human eyes) increased further with his resurrection, and culminated in his ascension to the right hand of God. The final stage of Jesus' glorification was witnessed first by Stephen, then by Saul of Tarsus, then by John.

The apostle John has been widely recognised as the author of the Book of Revelation since the beginning of the second century. He describes what he saw in a vision:

> I turned round to see the voice that was
> speaking to me, and saw someone "like
> a son of man" dressed in a robe reaching
> down to his feet and with a golden sash
> round his chest. His head and hair were
> like wool, as white as snow, and his
> eyes were like blazing fire. His feet
> were like bronze glowing in a furnace,
> and his voice was like the sound of
> rushing waters. (Revelation 1.12-15).

This is reminiscent of the vision of Daniel several centuries before (Daniel 7.13-14). The vision of John, like that of Daniel, carries cosmic implications, regarding the one to whom has been given all authority and power over all things, peoples and nations. What is truly impressive about the present scene is that John is seeing the risen Jesus in his pre-existent glory. John is the only writer of the four Gospels who stresses at various moments the pre-existence of Jesus Christ. The first moment comes at the outset of his Gospel: "He was with God in the beginning." (John 1.2). John also opens his Gospel with the stupendous statement that at his incarnation, the pre-existent Christ and Jesus of Nazareth became *one: "And the Word became flesh."* (1.14). What is altogether amazing, though, is that they remained joined together, as one person, *after* his ascension, providing access to this heavenly state, for all human beings who place their hope and trust in him.

Jesus' post-resurrection body, though different, still bore the marks of crucifixion. It was *still* a human body.

Jesus: Dead or Alive?

Then came the final transformation. For lack of richer seams of language to describe this new reality, now *quite different*, but not totally *other*, John can only describe this as vital and awesome, possessing the elements, critical for life, of blazing fire and rushing water (1.14-15). No wonder he fell to the ground, as though dead (1.17). The one he saw was Jesus, *like he had never seen him before.*

Through a variety of situations and by way of individuals of contrasting personality, background and circumstance, we are drawn to the unmistakeable conclusion that the *glory* of the Christ, once veiled in human flesh, is no longer veiled. Peter alludes to the unveiled, *heavenly* glory of Jesus, in his address to the crowd in Jerusalem, when he says: "The God of Abraham, Isaac and Jacob, the God of our fathers, has glorified his servant Jesus." (Acts 3.13). This is an allusion to his post-ascension glory, or his elevation to the highest place in heaven. This is the underlying theme of Jesus' personal prayer to the Father: "And now, Father, glorify me in your presence with the glory I had with you before the world began." (John 17.5). Here, in particular, we have a sense of the pre-incarnate glory of Jesus, of which he divested himself at his coming into the world, and into which he enters again on the occasion of his ascension to heaven. To use an analogy; if we think of morning light before the sun has risen above the horizon, we can see its light, but not its disc. That would be to compare it with Jesus' body before his resurrection. If, then, we think of the sun veiled behind high cloud, when we can see its pale disc and look straight into it. That would be to compare it with Jesus body after his resurrection, during the forty days before the

Ascension. Then to see him after the forty days can be likened to the midday sun, high above the horizon, in blazing light. The sun's disc is lost in the intensity of its own light and we are unable to look directly into it. The risen Lord is now exalted to the right hand of God and, to use the words of the hymn writer, "hid from our sight in inaccessible light." But we shall see his glory, fully and perfectly revealed, when we are raised a spiritual body, clothed in a body fit for heaven (1 Corinthians 15.44).

Now, in the post-Pentecost era of God's timeline, his presence is with us through the Holy Spirit. John *also* wrote of this: "The world cannot accept him, because it neither sees him nor knows him. But you know him, for he lives with you and will be in you." (14.17). John also makes an explicit connection between the resurrection, ascension and the receiving of the Holy Spirit at Pentecost (16.7). These three events in God's timeline are strategically connected, the one being dependent on the other. It is God's purpose that we should experience his continuing activity, though this is no longer mediated through the *historical Jesus*, who once walked on earth.

Jesus makes an extraordinary prediction concerning the fall and rise of the Jerusalem Temple, which is recorded in the Fourth Gospel (2.19). This prediction follows on from the so-called cleansing of the Temple, when Jesus overthrew the tables of the moneychangers. John places this at the *beginning* of Jesus' ministry, though the prediction clearly relates to his dying and rising again at the *close* of his earthly ministry. Answering a question from the Jews about his authority to act as he did in relation to the Temple, Jesus challenges them to destroy it, but then makes what seems an audacious claim to be able to rebuild it in three days. This is clearly figurative language, on the part of Jesus, and refers to his death at the hands of men and his resurrection by the power of God. Interestingly, in the synoptic gospels, this same event is placed at the beginning of the week leading up to the *crucifixion*, but in all four Gospels, it takes place in the days leading up to the annual *Passover festival.* We may be looking at the same *unique event* as recorded in the synoptic gospels, but for editorial reasons John places it at the beginning of Jesus' ministry. In this case, it sets the tone for Jesus' ministry as a whole, and is in keeping with the distinctive theological approach to the life and ministry of Jesus taken by this gospel writer. There may, of course, have been *two such events*, one at the beginning and the other at the end of Jesus' ministry, though the present writer is of the opinion that it is one and the same event and that, *historically,* it belongs at the beginning of what is known as 'Holy Week'.

In relation to the resurrection appearances of Jesus, the connection we are invited to make (the logical connection), is between the Temple and the resurrection body of Jesus. The Temple was revered by the Jews as the place of God's dwelling, in particular the area of the Temple behind the curtain, to which only the High Priest was allowed access on the Day of Atonement. With this in mind, the resurrection body of Jesus becomes the seat of God's life and presence on earth, in a way far more accentuated than before the Resurrection.

Chapter Three

The first-hand witnesses

Never was there a more varied group of people, different in personality and temperament. These are the principal witnesses insofar as we know more about them and the circumstances in which they saw Jesus after his resurrection. We are, therefore, able to test out their accounts of the Resurrection, compare them and use them to form a picture of events as related in all four Gospels.

Mary Magdalene was from the town of Magdala, on the western shore of the sea of Galilee. She was the first witness to the resurrection of Jesus. Mary was a loyal follower of Jesus and deeply devoted to him. We are told that he had delivered her from seven demons, or as David Catchpole puts it: "a release from total control by demonic forces" (*Resurrection People,* p. 105). No more than any of the other followers of Jesus, she did not expect to see him again after his burial, at which she herself had been present, together with the other women from Galilee (Matthew 27.61; Mark 15.47; Luke 23.55). Tearfully, she mistook him for the gardener working in the vicinity of the tomb, in the early morning light of that first Easter Sunday. This was the second time she had visited the tomb on that first Easter Sunday morning. On the first occasion we are given the impression in the Johannine tradition, that she went to the tomb alone. Is there a major discrepancy here between the synoptic accounts and that of John? No. Frank Morison, with his usual journalistic attention to detail, makes the following incisive observation:

> It is not the custom of the writer of the Fourth Gospel to be intentionally obscure or confusing when describing matters of fact. On the contrary, his work contains examples of some of the most lucid and vivid descriptive writing in literature. He commands a literary technique capable of expressing the most delicate nuances of meaning and he almost invariably uses it to produce an impression of pellucid clarity. But in this passage, whether from a momentary inattention or because the subject of Mary's friends did not seem to him important, he has achieved one of the outstanding literary examples of obscurity in the Gospels. He begins by describing Mary's departure for the tomb at a time when few people would be about unless they had risen with the intention of accompanying her. He describes her as running back in a state of great excitement to tell Peter and John, and he records what is clearly a deeply imprinted recollection of her breathless and historic utterance: "They have taken away the Lord, and we do

not know where they have laid him."
Why this incomprehensible "we" if it
was not part of his understanding of the
matter that Mary did not go unattended
and that she was reporting what she had
found, or rather failed to find, in
company with others? *(Who Moved the
Stone?* pp. 73-74).

Furthermore, the detail in the story reveals one other
interesting probability: 'the other disciple' was more than
likely to have been John, himself, as is often assumed, even
by Morison. The reason the other women are not
mentioned is that John was focusing primarily on the
report given to him personally by Mary Magdalene. It was
Mary who had given the report, so it would be natural for
him to refer to her as the one who went to the tomb. But
the outstanding feature of Mary's report is that she still
thought Jesus was dead. So far as she was concerned, the
explanation was simple: his body had been *removed from
the tomb*. Though recognition was slow, on her second visit
to the tomb, she did recognise his voice when he spoke her
name. It was in the familiar words and gestures that Jesus
was recognised, not only by Mary, but by the two disciples
on the road to Emmaus; and also, by John, on a Galilean
fishing trip, two thousand years ago.

The other women. These are Mary the mother of
James, Salome and Joanna. Mary the mother of James has
been identified as the mother of James the son of Alphaeus,
one of the twelve disciples. Salome is thought to be the
wife of Zebedee and, therefore, the mother of James and

Jesus: Dead or Alive?

John. She may also have been the sister of Jesus' mother, both of whom were among the women who witnessed the crucifixion (John 19.25). Joanna was the wife of an important official at Herod's court, and one of the women, including Mary Magdalene and Mary the mother of James, who supported Jesus' ministry, providing for him and the disciples out of their means (Luke 8.2-3). In Matthew's Gospel we are told that two women went to the tomb on Easter Sunday morning, namely, Mary Magdalene and the other Mary. Mark, the earliest written narrative, informs us that there were three women, Mary Magdalene, Mary the mother of James and Salome. Luke, on the other hand, records that it was Mary Magdalene, Joanna and Mary the mother of James, and some others. John reports that only Mary Magdalene went to the tomb. Mark and Luke tell us that the women took spices to anoint the body of Jesus, whereas Matthew and John do not mention this. Mary Magdalene is the only woman to appear in all four accounts.

Peter was the leader of the twelve disciples of Jesus. However, he was an impetuous and impulsive man. He would rush in, as we say, where angels fear to tread. For example, on the Mount of the Transfiguration, of the three disciples who witnessed this moment, it was Peter who impulsively suggested that they built three booths, one for Moses, another for Elijah and one for Jesus. He was an uneducated fisherman, in the sense that he had received little or no formal education. We would say today, that he had been educated in the university of life. At the trial of Jesus before the Sanhedrin, Peter was unnerved by the questions directed towards him from those gathered around

58

the fire outside the house of Caiaphas, which led to his denial that he knew Jesus or had any part in his ministry. The post-resurrection accounts suggest that he was the first of the eleven to whom Jesus appeared and, more than the others, he would have been in need of reassurance and forgiveness for his actions in denying Jesus, not once but three times, when accused of being one his disciples on the night before the crucifixion.

John is known to have had a quick temper like his brother James (Jesus called them the 'Sons of Thunder', see Mark 3.17). However, John clearly had another side to his personality and was perceptive in many ways, and quite the opposite to Peter. He was reflective and abounding in spiritual and theological insights, reminiscent of the Gospel that bears his name. John was the youngest of the disciples and a cousin of Jesus; his mother and Mary, the mother of Jesus, as we have already seen, were probably sisters. It was to John, in fact, to whom Jesus entrusted the care of his mother at the cross. The actions and reactions of John and Peter are portrayed perfectly in the gospels and so true to character; in particular, in relation to the resurrection appearances of Jesus. The impetuous, impulsive nature of the one, and the perceptive, insightful nature of the other, is clear to see both at the empty tomb and on the Sea of Galilee. John arrives first at the tomb, he looks in, but does not enter the tomb. Peter catches up with him and rushes straight in, wondering what had happened. John then enters the tomb and *believes*. On their fishing trip in Galilee, John is the first to recognise Jesus on the shore. But it is Peter who, unable to wait for the boat to arrive, plunges into the water, in order to swim to the shore and reach Jesus in the quickest possible time. Both John and Peter acted according to what we already know about their individual personalities, with nothing contrived or imagined by the writer of these two resurrection narratives.

Thomas is the disciple for whom seeing is believing. However, according to Jesus, believing gives us the ability to *see*: "Blessed are they who believe, who have not seen" (with their physical eyes). Thomas has received a bad press over the years, and is known as 'Thomas the Doubter', the principal example of all who doubt that Jesus is alive today. Tradition informs us that he went on to become a missionary to India, and like ten of the eleven apostles, was martyred for the sake of Jesus Christ. Thomas's confession, 'My Lord and my God', is similar to that of Peter's at Caesarea Philippi, on the slopes of Mount Hermon. It is an admission of the divine as well as human nature of Jesus.

James. After the Resurrection, Jesus also appeared to his brother, James (not to be confused with James the son of Zebedee and brother of John). We are told about this by the apostle Paul (1 Corinthians 15.7), quoting perhaps the earliest credal document of the church, though he gives no insight as to where and when Jesus appeared to James. I have advanced a hypothesis in Chapter 5 with regard to the appearance of the risen Lord to James, based on a fragment from the Gospel of the Hebrews. Paul informs us that James was *among the first* to whom Jesus appeared after his resurrection. However, the above-mentioned fragment suggests that he may have been *the first* of those who were to be the basis of the primitive church, to whom Jesus appeared after his resurrection. We do know that

The first-hand witnesses

James became a prominent figure in the Jerusalem church and possibly the recognised leader of the Christian community there, which might have afforded him priority among those who saw the risen Christ. He was not one of the eleven, but, in fact, an outsider at this point. It is known from the Gospels that James, along with his siblings, were sceptical towards their brother and his itinerant ministry in Galilee. The sense of this is given in the Gospel of Mark: "Then Jesus entered a house, and again a crowd gathered, so that he and his disciples were not even able to eat. When his family heard about this, they went to take charge of him, for they said, 'He is out of his mind.' " (3.20-21). A similar impression regarding the relationship of Jesus to his family is given in the following reaction towards his blood family: "My mother and brothers are they who hear God's word and put it into practice." (Luke 8.19-21). It is interesting that the importance of being doers of God's word and not only hearers, is central to the New Testament letter of James, which is generally recognised as having been written by the Lord's brother.

There is also good evidence from extra-biblical literature (Josephus, Origen and Eusebius), that James, the leader of the Jerusalem church, was the brother of Jesus, called the Christ, and that having given his allegiance to the church he died as a martyr for his part in it. Paul on a visit to Jerusalem, following his own conversion, tells us that he met Peter and no other among the apostles except James, the brother of the Lord, an allusion to the important role that James had within the church of that city.

Jesus: Dead or Alive?

Understanding their stories

These are a cross-section of personalities, some as different as chalk is from cheese (in the case of Peter and John). They would not have *all* been tricked into believing that Jesus had risen from the dead. John Stott brings out a trait in the women who went to the tomb and their approach to the task of anointing the body of Jesus: "They had brought spices and were going to complete the anointing of their Lord's body, since the approach of the sabbath had made the work so hasty two days previously. These devoted and business-like women were not the kind to be easily deceived or to give up the task they had come to do." (*Basic Christianity*, p. 48, cited in Josh McDowell, *Evidence that Demands a Verdict,* p. 258). I refer to this because it is a trait that I have often seen among *donas de casa* (housewives) in Brazil. It is also one which I can mirror in the action and reaction of these Jewish women.

There were, as we have seen from the different accounts of the Resurrection, points at which they disagreed; we are even presented with the disbelief of the disciples (Luke 24.11). However, Peter wasted no time in going to the tomb to see for himself (24.12). That the tomb was empty was beyond doubt. What no one had an answer for was the whereabouts of the body of Jesus. As evening fell, the disciples (apart from Thomas) were together behind locked doors for fear of the Jews. After all, they would have been suspected of removing the body of Jesus, which is exactly the story that the religious authorities had put around. This is the same as Nero blaming the Christians for setting fire to Rome. The disciples of Jesus were naturally keeping a low profile, at least until the whole episode had blown over. But the resolution to the matter was very different from what even the disciples could have imagined.

We know from the Gospel of Luke that Peter went to the tomb to verify the women's story, and the Gospel of John informs us that both Peter and John did the same thing, with the added detail that John, who was younger, outran Peter and arrived first, though he did not immediately enter the tomb. Peter, on the other hand, did. Eventually, John, who had arrived first went into the tomb. There is an interesting comment made by the evangelist who says that finally John entered the tomb, saw and believed, though neither of the two understood that in Scripture this had been foretold (John 20.9). The same lack of understanding is also found in the disciples whom Jesus met on the road to Emmaus that same Sunday evening. Why did Jesus draw alongside these two, if not to reassure them? His resurrection was not a figment of their imagination; the evidence in no way suggests this. To say otherwise, distorts the facts and the experience of Jesus' followers. The evidence always points to the real, the physical and, yes, the unbelievable. Initially, there was genuine perplexity on the part of those who had known Jesus before his crucifixion, as to what was happening. The story also contains detail which reflects accurately characteristics of the two disciples who went to the tomb on hearing the women's report. As the story unfolds, differences will naturally appear in the way different people remember the events. There is no evidence that the storytellers made a concerted effort to fabricate the essential facts.

The appearances of Jesus are evidence of his rising from the dead. But these appearances are subject to analysis and scrutiny. What kind of appearances were they? If we conclude that they were simply the product of the disciples' creative or overactive imaginations, we should remember that this illusion was replicated many times, by different people in different places and situations. And, after all, the disciples did not expect Jesus to rise from the dead, even though he had explained this to them at Caesarea Philippi, when he set his face resolutely towards Jerusalem. Would such strivings of human imagination and desire have even been possible, let alone sufficient to carry the disciples through opposition, persecution and the constant threat of torture and execution? Just think of the two deeply despondent figures returning to Emmaus at sunset on that first Easter Sunday. The sun was setting not only in the western sky, but also on all their hopes that Jesus was the promised Jewish Messiah. For how long, is it reasonable to believe, would such a tenuous hold on tattered hopes have sustained them and the future church?

Chapter Four

Biblical and secular evidence

As we have already observed, there are undeniable divergencies between the different accounts of the Resurrection appearances of Jesus. Perhaps the inherent problem is that we have four Gospel traditions and not one. Though we are enriched by having more information about the life, death, resurrection and ascension of Jesus from the different records, there will always be some differences in the way the story is told and recalled. This is true of any multiple retelling of a story, and should not surprise us, and neither should it bring into serious doubt the points at which the storytellers are all agreed.

The narratives

The Gospel writers do nothing to try and persuade or condition us to believe that Jesus rose from the dead. They certainly do not attempt to cover up the initial unbelief of the disciples on receiving the women's report. At first, the disciples, themselves, received with incredulity the report that he had risen from the dead. Though the details differ between the four Gospel accounts, there is total agreement that Jesus rose from the dead. Between his resurrection and ascension, Jesus appeared on ten separate occasions to different people, men and women, individually and in groups. Firstly, he appeared to Mary Magdalene at the tomb; secondly, to the women returning from the empty tomb. Then he appeared to Peter and after that to two disciples on the road to Emmaus. He then appeared to the disciples in the Upper Room on Easter Sunday. A week later he appeared to the eleven, including Thomas, and later to seven of the disciples on the shores of Galilee. Before the close of the forty days, he appeared again in Galilee at a mountain where he commissioned the disciples to their world-wide mission. He also appeared to James, his brother, who later became leader of the Jerusalem church. And, lastly, on the Mount of Olives, in Jerusalem, on the occasion of his ascension.

That the apostles witnessed the Resurrection is confirmed in connection with the choice of a successor to Judas Iscariot. Peter, who initiates the process of drawing by lots, made it mandatory that the shortlist should contain the names only of those from among their number who had witnessed the events surrounding the life, death and resurrection of Jesus (Acts 1.21-26). Unless the disciples had seen the risen Jesus, and not just an empty tomb (which, in itself, would not have proved the Resurrection to be a fact), instead of preoccupying themselves with electing Matthias to replace Judas Iscariot, they would have remained quietly behind bolted doors until the whole episode had passed into history.

Why do we need to hear about this? I was once asked this question by a young person at a church in London after the Easter morning sermon. I think that she felt it was enough to proclaim the Resurrection without going into all the details as to why we can trust the early traditions regarding this event. She is, of course, right. It should not be necessary to continue giving proofs for something which is transparently clear. The fact that the church exists at all is amazing. The renowned Scottish theologian, James Denney, considers that the whole of the New Testament is proof of the Resurrection; the evidence of faith and transformed lives, of lives laid down in the name of Jesus. It is true that one might give their life for a lie, believing that it was true. But no one would do this knowing that it was a lie. The only explanation for the continuing witness of the apostles and the New Testament church is that the message of the Resurrection is wholly true. This message has continued to be preached down the centuries for the simple reason that it is *true*. In fact, it requires less mental gymnastics to believe that it is true than to believe otherwise. So that young lady was right. The evidence stands on its own feet, without any external assistance.

A. M. Ramsey, in his book *The Resurrection of Christ*, makes the following observations about the Resurrection in the synoptic gospels:

> Luke's narratives of the Resurrection diverge from Mark to a greater extent than do Matthew's, both in literary sources and in theological themes. If Mark shows us the Resurrection as the breaking into history of a transcendental act of God, Luke shows rather the place of the Resurrection

Jesus: Dead or Alive?

within that process of history wherein
the purpose of God is unfolded. (p. 78).

These differences do not undermine the historicity
of the events described. Rather they exist to allow us to
contemplate the Resurrection from a variety of different
angles and appreciate the height, breadth and depth of
God's action in Jesus Christ. Mark states the plain facts,
while Luke goes further and begins to interpret those facts,
creating a kind of bridge between the synoptic gospels and
the Gospel of John, who (after another half-century
processing all this) is able to draw out deeper theological
conclusions pertaining to the life, death and resurrection of
Jesus Christ. If we are to remain objective in our reading
of the different texts, we should not allow variations of
detail to distract our attention from that which they have in
common and upon which they are all agreed.

Flavius Josephus

Some question the very existence of Jesus in order to
resolve the problem of his resurrection. For those who for
whatever reason do not wish to deposit confidence in the
biblical account, we can turn to secular literature from a
time very close to the events recorded in the Gospels.
Flavius Josephus, was a first century Jewish historian (37
– 100 AD) and writes that Jesus was a virtuous man who
performed signs and wonders among the people, that he
was condemned to death and crucified. The relevant
historical text reads as follows:

Biblical and secular evidence

About this time there lived Jesus, a wise man. For he was one who performed surprising deeds and was a teacher of such people as accept the truth gladly. He won over many Jews and many of the Greeks. And when, upon the accusation of the principal men among us, Pilate had condemned him to a cross, those who had first come to love him did not cease. And the tribe of the Christians, so called after him, has still to this day not disappeared. *(Antiquities of the Jews,* Book 18.3.3).

This does not provide further evidence of the Resurrection of Jesus, but it does confirm that a man called Jesus was crucified under the orders of Pontius Pilate, the senior Roman representative in the region at the time. Explicit references to Jesus' resurrection, found in an alternative text, are omitted here, as they are considered to be interpolations attributed to the early church, as also is an affirmation that he was the promised Messiah.

In a tenth century Arabic manuscript of Josephus, the following is written, which closely resembles the original Josephus testimony, but with neutral references to the person of Jesus and his resurrection:

At this time there was a wise man who was called Jesus. And his conduct was good, and [he] was known to be virtuous. And many people from among

Jesus: Dead or Alive?

> the Jews and the other nations became
> his disciples. Pilate condemned him to
> be crucified and to die. And those who
> had become his disciples did not
> abandon his discipleship. They reported
> that he had appeared to them three days
> after his crucifixion and that he was
> alive. Accordingly, he was perhaps the
> Messiah concerning whom the prophets
> have recounted wonders.

Understandably, scholars do not consider it likely that a Jewish non-Christian historian would have used terms that express belief in the Resurrection or refer to Jesus as the Messiah. But even when the overtly Christian tones are stripped back, the evidence for the existence of Jesus, crucified under Pontius Pilate, is still laid bare.

Josephus also refers to "the brother of Jesus, who was called Christ, whose name was James" (*Antiquities, Book* 20.9.1). This corroborates the New Testament evidence that James was the brother of Jesus. For this reason, we can now build a solid argument to the effect that Jesus of Nazareth existed. Claims to his resurrection on the part of his followers, although alluded to, are not affirmed by Josephus, who was not born until four years *after* the event.

Our purpose in using the Josephus testimony is to establish as objectively as possible from ancient records that Jesus, known as the Christ, lived and died and was reported by his followers to have risen from the dead after

70

Biblical and secular evidence

three days in the tomb. There are different accounts as to the detail, but both the biblical and extra-biblical evidence support the fact that Jesus existed, and they also agree as to the events that have become central to the Christian faith through two thousand years.

If the records of a Jewish historian provide evidence that Jesus existed, that he was crucified under Pontius Pilate in the Roman province of Judea (as they do), then we have the ability to locate him in time and space. We know that Pilate was governor of Judea between AD 26 and AD 36. Of this we can be as certain as anything we read in the history books relating to that period of time. Wilhelm Vischer makes an interesting and pertinent remark in this respect:

> Jesus life from his birth under the rule of Augustus up to his execution under Pontius Pilate is a historical event; more precisely, an event of the history of Israel. The acknowledgement of this fact does not require belief in Jesus as the Christ. But neither does the Christian faith imply the denial of this fact, nor the need for declaring it irrelevant. ('Everywhere the Scripture is about Christ alone', in: The Old Testament and Christian Faith, p. 97).

To acknowledge that Jesus existed and lived in Palestine 2000 years ago is not necessarily an expression of faith in his person and work, or a personal commitment to his cause. But neither is Christian faith something solely of the here and now without its rootedness in history. The two (history and faith) can be separated and studied as two distinct disciplines, though the bigger picture is only seen when we bring the two *together*. Christian faith is founded on a past event, but lived as a contemporary experience of the Living One, who though he was dead is alive forevermore. (Revelation 1.18).

Cornelius Tacitus and Pliny the Younger

We have it that there is sufficient Jewish evidence outside the Bible to confirm that Jesus did exist and that he was crucified under the Roman regional governor, Pontius Pilate. We also have at our disposal the following on the authority of the Roman senator and historian, Tacitus:

> Nero looked around for a scapegoat, and inflicted the most fiendish tortures on a group of persons already hated for their crimes. This was the sect known as Christians. Their founder, one Christus, had been put to death by the procurator, Pontius Pilate in the reign of Tiberius. *(Annals*, Book 15.44).

It is remarkable that Pilate is best known in history because of his dealings with Jesus of Nazareth. If it had not been for Jesus, the world might never have heard of Pontius Pilate. So, in response to those who deny the evidence, we could ask if they accept the same evidence

Biblical and secular evidence

for the prefect of the Roman province of Judea? It is reasonable to argue, therefore, that as the crucifixion of a certain Jesus called 'Christus' is attested to in these secular historical documents, there is clear, if scarce, *extra-biblical* evidence for the existence of Jesus. This evidence is on a par with the evidence for the existence of the Emperor Nero, whose name appears in the very same document.

Of course, some may ask from whom did Tacitus get his information about the crucifixion of Jesus? I have heard it argued that if it were from the Christians in Rome, this would not be a sufficiently reliable source as to prove beyond reasonable doubt that Jesus existed. But there is no proof that it was the Christians alone from whom Tacitus was able to construct his history concerning Judea at the time of Jesus. Roman officials were also there, including those who carried out the act of crucifixion. A note of this event would have been kept in the official imperial records, to which Tacitus was given access. Tacitus was not particularly sympathetic towards the Christians, and we certainly have no indication that he was *biased* towards them. On occasion, in fact, he speaks harshly of the Christians:

> Christus, from whom the name (Christian) had its origin, suffered the extreme penalty during the reign of Tiberius at the hands of one of our procurators, Pontius Pilatus, and a most mischievous superstition, thus checked for the moment, again broke out not only in Judea, the first source of the

73

evil, but even in Rome, where all things hideous and shameful from every part of the world find their centre and become popular. (*Annals,* Book 15.44).

Furthermore, Tacitus was a highly respected historian for whom objectivity and a critical evaluation of the reports he received (and their sources) would have been paramount. It would be unusual if he did not check out his sources. The idea that he gleaned this information only from the Christians in Rome could be enough to discredit the historical fact of the crucifixion of Jesus. But if his methodology (in this particular respect) was not entirely scientific, it would discredit much else of what Tacitus wrote of the period from Tiberius to Nero.

Lastly, I refer to a letter written to the Emperor Trajan, in AD 112, by the Roman governor of Bithynia, Pliny the Younger. Pliny was seeking advice on how to deal with the numerous Christians in his province and their practices:

They were in the habit of meeting on a certain fixed day before it was light, when they sang an anthem to Christ as God, and bound themselves by a solemn oath *(sacramentum)* not to commit any wicked deed, but to abstain from all fraud, theft and adultery, never to break their word, or deny a trust when called upon to honour it; after which it was their custom to separate, and then

Biblical and secular evidence

meet again to partake of food, but food of an ordinary and innocent kind. (*Epistles* x. 96, cited by F. F. Bruce in *The New Testament Documents,* p. 119).

This document from a Roman governor to his Emperor is further incontrovertible evidence from *non-Christian* writings of the historical existence of Jesus Christ. It also supports the historical reliability of the *Christian* traditions, so often, so easily dismissed.

Chapter Five

A closer look at the events

By the time the women reached the tomb at first light, the stone had been removed from the entrance. This happened, I would argue, for the sake of the visitors to the tomb, not so that Jesus could walk out of it. Later that day, we know that he appeared to his disciples in the Upper Room, though the door was bolted fast 'for fear of the Jews.' The significance of this observation has to do with the changed nature of the physical body of Jesus. This different kind of body is not only plausible, but necessary for a coherent understanding of the post-resurrection appearances of Jesus between Easter Sunday and the Ascension. David Catchpole explains this new reality: "He can participate in the world of space and time, but he is not bound by it." (*Resurrection People,* p. 127). It also has repercussions for Paul's teaching about the resurrection body. What happened to Jesus in the past is key to our own future. We shall now have a closer look at events and issues relating to the empty tomb.

The wrong tomb

The written accounts have been subject to a good deal of historical and literary criticism, as has the story's inherent credibility. For example, in Mark's account of the resurrection, it has been suggested that the women went to the wrong tomb, but were then directed to the right one by the young man they had met there (Professor K. Lake, *The Historical Evidence for the Resurrection of Jesus Christ,* cited by A. M. Ramsey, *The Resurrection of Christ*). This interpretation is based on the words of the young man, dressed in white, at the empty tomb, in Mark's account of the Resurrection: "He is not here. See the place where they laid him." This is a classic example of quoting out of context and conveniently skips over the preceding words of the young man: "You are looking for Jesus the Nazarene, who was crucified. He has risen!" In fairness, one should always look at every piece of the evidence.

This is the story as we have it: Mary Magdalene witnessed the crucifixion together with Mary the mother of James and of Joses (a variant of Joseph), and Salome (Mark 15.40). It has been variously suggested and denied that the second Mary was Mary the mother of Jesus, as two of his brothers were called James and Joses (Mark 6.3). However, this is unlikely, as it would have been more natural for her to be referred to as 'Mary the mother of Jesus', or for her to have been placed first in order of names. We are also informed that Mary Magdalene and Mary the mother of Joses were present at the burial of Jesus and (significantly, in view of the 'wrong tomb theory') the closing of the tomb (15.47). To this last detail, Mark appears to draw special attention, perhaps anticipating the later emergence of a 'wrong tomb theory'. We know, too, that Mary Magdalene went to the tomb on Easter Sunday morning with Mary the mother of James, and Salome (16.1). From this we are able to gather that Mary

A closer look at the events

Magdalene and Mary the mother of James and Joses were, in fact, present at the crucifixion of Jesus, his burial, and at the empty tomb. It would be improbable that these two women, who had *together* witnessed the burial, would have *both* mistaken the tomb in which the body of Jesus had been laid a mere thirty-six hours before. It is also worth bearing in mind that these two women were the *only* people present at *all* three stages of this world-changing event, two thousand years ago.

The message given to the women by the young man conveys the facts very clearly: "He is not here" (Mark 16.6); not because it was the wrong tomb, but because he had risen. And if that young man *had* been indicating another tomb in which the body of Jesus had been laid, the body would have been found soon enough, once the women had been directed to the right tomb. However hard one may argue for a so-called rational explanation the clamour of truth will not go away.

The servant of the priest

I mentioned earlier that Frank Morison in *Who Moved the Stone?* uses an apocryphal tradition, of which only a short portion survives today. From the Gospel of the Hebrews, he quotes a passage referring to 'the servant of the priest' and also to Jesus appearing to his brother, James. Here are the first lines of that passage: "Now the Lord, when he had given the linen cloth unto the servant of the priest, went unto James and appeared to him" (p. 190). There is an immediacy in relation to Jesus leaving the tomb and appearing to his brother James.

Jesus: Dead or Alive?

Although Morison does not claim any hard evidence as to who moved the stone, he does ask questions about the circumstances surrounding this whole event. Morison is highly sceptical of the presence of angels at the tomb, and does not see anything remotely supernatural in the presence of the young man who was inside the tomb, when the women arrived there. But the question remains: Is there a connection between the young man in the empty tomb and the servant of the priest? Also, is there a possible link between the servant of the priest in the tomb and the one whose severed ear Jesus restored in the Garden of Gethsemane? (Mark 14.47). Are they one and the same person? This servant might well have been sufficiently motivated as to visit Jesus' tomb in the early hours of that first Easter morning. After all, he had been the beneficiary of an extraordinary miracle, at a time when Jesus attention might otherwise have been given to more pressing matters. This may be speculative, but it cannot be ruled out. The pieces of the jigsaw are tantalisingly similar in shape and size to those required to form this exact picture, and at the very least warrant keeping an open mind. Morison, having looked here and there for an answer, asks this question: "What, then, are we to make of that curious and significant sentence which describes Jesus as giving 'the linen cloth to the servant of the priest?' Is this a complete invention, a flight of fancy, or are we here right back in some vaguely remembered detail of the original night?" He then issues this challenge: "I will venture to warn the reader not to return too hasty an answer" (p. 191).

For those who have difficulty with the supernatural, 'the servant of the priest', as described in the Gospel of the

A closer look at the events

Hebrews, or, alternatively, the 'young man' as portrayed in Mark's Gospel might be a more realistic option than the angelic figures described in the other Gospels. It is fairly obvious, however, that a single human would not have been able to remove the heavy stone (placed, as it was, in a downward sloping groove) on their own. But other more pressing questions arise as to how the stone was moved. To be truthful, we really don't know the answer to this, the greatest of all mysteries. Morison has to concede at this point, so effectively fails to answer the question posed in the title of his best-selling book. But then, we may be barking up the wrong tree. Let us pause for a moment and consider another line of investigation.

If James were the first person to whom Jesus revealed himself after the Resurrection, he may have gone to the tomb that morning to establish beyond doubt that the body of Jesus was not there, and to confirm that he had not merely imagined that Jesus had appeared to him. Such things do happen, of course, and I remember clearly my mother having seen her mother in the front room of our home some while after she had died. The memory of my grandmother was clearly still very vivid in my mother's mind. Let us imagine that James *had* asked for help from the guards in removing the stone. In this case, they would have seen that the body of Jesus was no longer there when they went inside the tomb. But I would rule this out on the grounds that the stone must have been removed already, in order for *the servant of the priest* to be able to enter the tomb. From whatever angle one looks at this situation, the evidence is unequivocal: by the time his followers arrived at the tomb, the body of Jesus was no longer there. Taking the Easter story as a whole, we are drawn towards this: that Jesus was able to vacate the tomb without the need for the stone to be removed from the entrance. As we shall see, this is well supported by the Matthean tradition, which clearly states that the angel rolled back the stone, *in the presence of* the women (and, of course, the terrorised guards), and then informed them (the women) that Jesus was no longer there, as he had *already risen.* This is what the text tells us: "There was a violent earthquake, for an angel of the Lord came down from heaven and, going to the tomb, *rolled back the stone* and sat on it. The angel said to the women, "Do not be afraid, for I know you are looking for Jesus who was crucified. He is not here; he has risen, just as he said. 'Come and see the place where he lay.' " (Matthew 28.1-6). Angelic beings apart, the stone was removed *after* Jesus had vacated the tomb, according to the Matthean tradition. This is also consistent with the nature and occasion of the subsequent resurrection appearances. Furthermore, as Morison points out, there is no mention whatsoever in any of the earliest traditions that Jesus moved the stone *himself.* So, when we gather all the evidence and piece it together, there remains only one explanation regarding the stone.

At this point, I should like to add an 'in parentheses' concerning the release of Peter from prison, which happened with the help of an angel. If it had not been for this miraculous intervention, Peter would have remained in prison to face his untimely demise. He was sleeping when this unusual escape plan began to take shape. Initially, Peter was confused by what was happening (so who ever told the story must have heard it from Peter, to have known

A closer look at the events

what was going on in Peter's mind at the time). The angel led the way, passing the prison guards, until they reached the main gate, which apparently *opened by itself.* The apostle then made his way to the house where the disciples usually met together (the house with the upper room, belonging to John Mark and his mother, Mary). On arriving there he knocked on the door (because, unlike Jesus after his resurrection, he had no special powers of entry). When he called out, the servant girl, Rhoda, was overjoyed that it was Peter at the door. Without opening the door, she ran back into the house with the news. However, the group that was praying for his safe release from prison *did not believe* that it could be Peter. On the insistence of Rhoda, they concluded that it was his angel, thus assuming he had already been executed. Eventually, they opened the door and were astonished to see Peter (Acts 12.1-19). Whenever a turn of events was influenced by the supernatural, the fledgling church was consistent in *refusing to believe* the reports it was hearing, or in this case, an outcome it was praying for. The same lack of belief applied to the Resurrection of Jesus. There is no attempt by the writer to hide or exaggerate the facts. To the contrary, only to tell it as it *actually happened.*

Other than the fact he rose from the dead, there is no logical explanation as to why the body of Jesus was no longer in the tomb. If the disciples had stolen it, why did Peter and 'the other disciple' rush to the tomb to check out the report brought to them by the women? If the tomb had been mistaken, why was the right tomb not found and the body produced, in order to put an end to the matter? This would have been relatively easy to do, and there were enough people in high places, with a vested interest in disproving the Resurrection, to insist that this was done at the earliest opportunity.

The significance of the grave clothes

One other aspect of the empty tomb requires closer attention. The reference to the position of the grave clothes must be significant in some way. If the body of Jesus had been taken from the tomb, why not take it with the grave clothes? Why take the trouble to remove them from the body? If it were grave robbers, they would have been in a hurry. If it were the disciples, no less so. The arrangement of the linen strips suggests that Jesus' body had *changed*. The Lucan tradition concerning the place where the body had been laid indicates that the grave clothes were *undisturbed* (Luke 24.12). In John's Gospel the burial cloth that had been around Jesus' head was folded up by itself, separate from the linen (John 20.6-7). This would point to an orderly and purposeful vacating of the tomb. Whatever we conclude from the arrangement of the grave clothes, they had served their purpose and were of no further use. There is a strong sense that the period between Easter and the Ascension was a time of transition. This transition happened in three phases: the first, on Easter Sunday; the second, forty days later, when Jesus last appeared to his disciples; the third, on the Day of Pentecost. As human beings we rely on time-space concepts to understand and interpret the world around us; in fact, these are the only concepts that are available to us. Even Albert Einstein could not escape this reality. It was, therefore, necessary for our understanding of the resurrection that the stone was removed. To our minds how else could Jesus have left the tomb? Of course, the stone was moved, but the question is, 'when and by whom'? As I have indicated already, it was not moved for Jesus' benefit, but for ours. Confirmation that the body was no longer there was critical to the belief that he had been raised from the dead (though, not in itself a proof of the Resurrection, only that Jesus was no longer in the tomb). The position of the grave clothes, however, is a key factor for our understanding of what happened on that first Easter Sunday. The evidence of the grave clothes points us in one direction and touches upon the matter of the stone. There was no need for someone to assist Jesus as he left the tomb, certainly not an angel, as in the garden of Gethsemane before the trial and crucifixion (Luke 22.43). If we isolate the different aspects of the Resurrection, we are left with fragments of the story. But if we bring the pieces together, they form a picture and we are able to grasp the fact that the story is entirely plausible, at the very least. When John looked into the empty tomb, he *saw* the grave clothes (John 20.5); but when he entered the tomb, he saw and *believed* (20.8). There has been considerable discussion as to what we should understand by the words: 'he saw and believed'. The problem has been in connection with their *continued lack of understanding*. Did John merely believe what Mary Magdalene had told them, that the body of Jesus had been removed from the tomb; or did he believe that Jesus had risen from the dead. If so, was it the arrangement of the grave clothes that caused him to believe? Great minds have disagreed on this matter, including the Early Church Fathers Augustine of Hippo and John Chrysostom. Augustine was of the former opinion, while Chrysostom was of the latter. Luther and John Wesley took the position of Augustine, while Calvin agreed with Chrysostom. My own inclination is to take the most natural meaning of the word, as it stands, without qualification; that is, John believed that Jesus had risen. There are two reasons that I would give for taking this position: firstly, it is consistent with John's use of the word 'believe' throughout his Gospel; secondly, the *lack of understanding* was in respect of how Jesus' resurrection had been foretold in Scripture; not that he had risen.

When was the stone moved?

It is consistent with the resurrection appearances to say, that when Jesus rose from the dead, he was able to leave the tomb without the necessity of removing the stone. This would be no more difficult than to enter a room via a closed and locked door, or to disappear from sight without being seen to leave, or as the result of physical movement. Exactly this happened on two separate occasions: firstly, at Emmaus, in the house of the two disciples, on their return home after the Feast of Passover. Secondly, in the Upper Room, that first Easter Sunday evening. Jesus' body had changed between Good Friday and Easter Sunday. He was no longer subject to the restrictions of a purely physical human body. Tom Wright, in his book, *Surprised by Hope*, says it was "a new *kind* of physical body which left the empty tomb behind it, because it had 'used up' the material of Jesus' original body, and which possessed new properties which nobody had expected or imagined…"

This would seem eminently compatible with the resurrection appearances in the Gospels of Luke and John. When Jesus left the tomb, he was clothed in a body that was still physical, but composed of significantly different material from ours or the one he had before he died.

This is demonstrated when Jesus appeared to his disciples on the shore of the Sea of Galilee, as recorded in John's Gospel. Tom Wright in a Veritas Forum interview observes the fact that the disciples dared not ask 'who are you?', because they knew it was the Lord (John 21.12). Wright explains that when someone is known to you, as the disciples were to Jesus, it would not be necessary to ask who it was when meeting that person again. The reason the Gospel writer includes this significant detail, is because the disciples perceived a physical change in Jesus. He was recognisable as the same person they had accompanied day by day for three years, but there was a difference, and they could not quite put their finger on it. Tom Wright concludes that because this is such a fascinating feature of the story, it would never have made up. The disciples were into new territory in terms of physical resurrection, and though it could not be explained, neither could it be explained *away*.

Are we not, therefore, on firmer ground by accepting the integrity of the story? Though a superficial observation might make that seem unlikely, it does merit closer inspection. It would appear that the Resurrection is more than wishful thinking on the part of this small group of followers; for some strange reason they were persuaded to believe that it was *true*.

Jesus: Dead or Alive?

The women's testimony

As we know, it was a group of women who first witnessed the empty tomb. However, the testimony of women in first century Israel was not considered to be reliable. Certainly, it was not admissible in a Jewish court of law. Josephus highlights this very different situation regarding women in his day compared to our own:

> But let not a single witness be credited, but three, or two at the least, and those such whose testimony is confirmed by their good lives. But let not the testimony of women be admitted, on account of the levity and temerity of their sex. Neither let slaves be admitted to give testimony, since it is probable that they will not speak the truth, either out of hope of gain, or fear of punishment. *(Antiquities*, Book 4.219).

Certainly, this attitude is reflected in the disciples' initial response to the news brought to them by the women, a connection David Catchpole has also made in his book, *Resurrection People,* pp. 200-201:

> Would anyone wishing to tell a convincing story have assigned the role of witnesses to a group of women? The instinct which caused Luke to superimpose a checking visit to the

88

tomb by Peter because the adequacy of the women is doubted, is exactly the instinct which would have kept the women out of any story created *ex nihilo* – and yet they are here! Not just here, but as a threesome described with such careful attention to detail that they cannot but be taken seriously as witnesses.

The Fourth Gospel also includes a 'checking visit' to the tomb by Peter and 'the other disciple', who ran together to the tomb, with exact details as to how that visit unfolded (John 20.3-9). If the disciples had stolen the body of Jesus, or removed it, or put it in another tomb, or whatever, would they have reacted in the way they did to the story told by the women? They would have already known what had happened to the body of Jesus, dispensing with the need for these theatrics.

It is also interesting to note that the early traditions place women quite specifically ahead of men when it comes to the appearances of Jesus. This would be like shooting oneself in the foot. Look at this piece of narrative from John's Gospel, written towards the end of the first century:

Then the disciples went back to their homes, but Mary stood outside the tomb crying. As she wept, she bent over to look into the tomb and saw two angels in white, seated where Jesus' body had

been, one at the head and the other at the
foot. They asked her, "Woman, why are
you crying?" "They have taken my
Lord away", she said, "and I don't know
where they have put him." At this, she
turned around and saw Jesus standing
there, but she did not realise that it was
Jesus. (John 20.10-14).

The point is this: if this story were written with the
hope of commanding some measure of credibility, Jesus
would have appeared while Peter and 'the other disciple'
were at the tomb; yet this didn't happen, at least not until
after they had left and Mary was alone. The narrative, as it
stands, depends on the testimony of a *solitary* witness not
two, and certainly not three, the preferred minimum
number required to substantiate a claim or charge in a legal
sense. And what is more, this witness was a *woman*, whose
testimony would not have been admitted in the first place.
Quite surely, the world should have heard nothing more
about Jesus of Nazareth. But the story has stood for two
thousand years, and no copyist or translator has ever
thought to change it.

Furthermore, the protagonists stood by Jesus to the
point of laying down their lives for him. That seems
incredible if it were all an act of stupendous deception.
James, the brother of Jesus, doubting Thomas and Saul of
Tarsus, would suffice to quell the notion of a resurrection,
if it were truly baseless. All of these were sceptics to the
point of hostility. To say they died for what was at best was

A closer look at the events

an unproven tale, or at worst a lie, would stretch the
imagination to its limits.

When did Jesus return to the Father?

This brings us to a further question as we look more closely
into the events surrounding the resurrection appearances of
Jesus. At what point during the forty days did Jesus return
to the Father? We know that Jesus' final appearance to his
disciples happened at the end of that period of time.
Because of our three-dimensional understanding of the
cosmos, our language is limited, and so we describe Jesus
as being 'taken up' into heaven. On that first Easter
morning, when Jesus spoke to Mary Magdalene at the
tomb, we are told that he resisted her attempts to *hold on*
to him, because he had not yet ascended to the Father. The
strength of the verb indicates 'to cling' 'hold on to', or
'embrace', rather than 'touch'. Such an action would have
hindered the process by which Jesus was ascending to the
Father. The following Sunday, Jesus invited Thomas to
reach out and *touch* the nail prints in his hands (or rather
his wrists). We should not read too much into these
comparisons, because of the difference in weight of the two
Greek verbs, which imply *different kinds* of action. The
action of *touching* was different from that of *clinging*. But
what is unmistakable is that Jesus' body had *significantly
changed* by the time he meets the disciples eight days after
the Resurrection. This is key to our understanding of the
Ascension and the time and manner of its occurrence. A.
M. Ramsey rightly observes that in John's Gospel, the
Ascension happened on Easter Day, and that in Luke's

91

Jesus: Dead or Alive?

Gospel, when Jesus is taken up into heaven, the disciples are given "a visible assurance that the appearances were ended." Of course, this is not to say that the Resurrection and the Ascension are one and the same thing. Rather they are two separate and distinguishable events, though closely related to each other (see Tom Wright, *Surprised by Hope,* p. 120). However, there are no clear lines of demarcation between the cross, the resurrection and the ascension, such that we can separate them in a linear time scheme.

The real significance of the ascension process is brought out by R.V.G Tasker in his commentary, *The Gospel According to St. John.*

> But the Son of God does not return to His Father exactly as He had come forth from the Father. Having taken upon Himself human nature He goes back with that human nature, still bearing the wounds inflicted upon Him when he was 'bruised for our iniquity.' (p. 222).

This lies at the heart of the redemptive action, wrought by God on behalf of the world; the marks of his rejection are still visible, but these marks have secured our reconciliation to God and our access to his eternal presence, beginning in the present age: "I am with you always." (Matthew 28.20).

A closer look at the events

Where is heaven?

Tom Wright speaks of heaven as the 'thin curtain' between God's space and ours (*Surprised by Hope,* p. 66). It is not a continuum of physical space as we know it. Yuri Gagarin, the first man in space, observed on his return to Earth that he had been to outer space and back and had not seen God. The same could be said for the Hubble Telescope or the Voyager II spacecraft, which is now well beyond the limits of our solar system. Even with the highest resolution cameras, there has been nothing to suggest the presence of a divine being out there. Of course, he could be invisible to human optical and digital technology, though strangely not to human eyes. So, we are left with three options: (1) God *is there,* but we cannot see him; (2) God *is not there* (or anywhere); (3) we are looking in the *wrong place.* I believe that heaven is much nearer than we think. That is why we can speak of God being closer to us than a brother; that he is around us and within us. As Paul said, quoting an ancient Greek poem: "In him we live and move and have our being." That is not to say that God is in all material things, as some philosophers have suggested. But neither is he distant and remote, uninterested in the lives of mere mortals. We usually refer to heaven as being '*up* in the sky'. But it is also all around us. The Christian experience of God is not *otherworldly* (or *detached* from this world), but *out of this world;* in other words, more wonderful than we can think or imagine. As in a jigsaw, the exact meaning of the individual pieces is only appreciated when they come together to form a complete picture. On the same plane, John's concept of 'eternal life' is not simply 'life without end', but 'life in all its fullness'. Perhaps there is more to the expression 'heaven on earth' than we have yet grasped.

This now brings us to the work of the Holy Spirit, by whom God's presence is mediated on earth. According to the Gospel of John, the receiving of the Holy Spirit by the disciples was conditional on Jesus returning to the Father. And in order for Jesus to return to the Father, he had to rise from the dead. This is the order of things both in the teaching of Jesus and in the narratives concerning Good Friday, Easter Sunday, the Ascension and Pentecost. After the Resurrection, Jesus appeared to his disciples and greeted them with the words, 'Peace be with you' and, also, 'Receive the Holy Spirit'. This he did on the first evening after the Resurrection. That is, of course, before his final appearance to them on the Mount of Olives at the end of the forty days. So, in fact, as Ramsey says, John wishes us to understand that the Ascension took place on Easter Day. The phenomena of 'a rushing wind' and 'tongues of fire' on the Day of Pentecost associated with the general outpouring of the Holy Spirit, as foretold by the prophet Joel, is not a problem in this context. The coming of the Holy Spirit, both in its general and restricted form, is the proof that Jesus rose from the dead and ascended to heaven.

The proof of who Jesus is and what he did

The Resurrection is also proof that the claims Jesus made about his person as the Son of God are indeed true, according to Paul's declaration to that effect in his letter to the Christian community in Rome: "who through the Spirit of holiness was declared with power to be the Son of God, by his resurrection from the dead." (Romans 1.4). The Resurrection is the vindication of the person of Jesus as the Son of God. In the light of his resurrection from the dead we are able to recognise his deity both in the nature of his being and the authority which he claimed to have received from God the Father, which we have on good account at his baptism in the river Jordan and at the Transfiguration in the presence of Moses and Elijah.

His resurrection also underpins the efficacy of his work on the cross. The two, his person and his work, are part and parcel. If he were not the incarnate God, he could not reconcile us to God. This we understand as the atonement, the bringing together of God and humanity into a renewed relationship. The incarnation and the atonement are essentially a single act on God's part, or a single event in human history. Jesus was born under the shadow of the cross. In a similar way, the empty tomb and the resurrection appearances of Jesus require each other. As Tom Wright points out, when taken together, they present irrefutable proof that Jesus did rise from the dead.

How far can the empty tomb and the appearances of Jesus, be verified historically? In our analysis and investigation, we shall allow the traditions of the empty tomb and the resurrection appearances to *guide* our thinking, in order to see where they take us. But to be certain that the *central elements* of the story are historically factual, we need to look at the *detail* within the story, which can be more illuminating than we sometimes imagine.

PART TWO

Assimilating the evidence

Chapter Six

In the Book of Acts

A major question and new instructions

Luke states clearly and unequivocally at the beginning of his second book (the Book of Acts), that Jesus revealed himself to the eleven after his resurrection, "and gave many convincing proofs that he was alive." (Acts 1.3). This he did over a period of forty days during which he spoke to them about the kingdom of God. In the interval between the Resurrection and the Ascension (the last post-resurrection appearance to the eleven disciples), Jesus met with them in Jerusalem and Galilee. It was during these times that Jesus continued to impart to the disciples his vision of the kingdom and prepare them for their future mission. It would seem that the disciples still had in mind an earthly kingdom and the restoration of the ancient Davidic line. The question vexing the minds of the disciples was when would he restore the kingdom to Israel? It was as if Jesus had been teasing this question out of the disciples during his ministry among them, particularly in his parables of the kingdom. Jesus replied to their question by telling them that not even he knew the answer; only the Father knows about the things that were of his sole prerogative. But he gave them an instruction as to what they should do in the immediate future, in the period between his ascension and the coming of the Holy Spirit. His instructions were to wait in Jerusalem until they had received power from on high (Acts 1.4). Forty days had already passed following the Resurrection, sufficient time for the disciples to assimilate the fact that Jesus was alive. Compare this period of time with other occurrences of 'Forty' in the Bible. The Flood (forty days and forty nights); the wilderness wanderings (forty years), the temptations of Jesus (forty days), the period between Palm Sunday, when Jesus wept over Jerusalem, and the destruction of Jerusalem. (AD 30 – AD 70). The time had come for a new moment in the lives of the disciples, something for which Jesus had carefully and patiently prepared them over the previous three years.

Peter, rushing in again!

He was then taken up into the clouds. There are parallels here with the Transfiguration when the cloud came down and covered Jesus, Moses and Elijah. After the cloud had lifted, only Jesus remained. This has theological implications, of course. Jesus incorporates and is superior to Moses and Elijah. He is the fulfilment of the Old Testament, the Law and the Prophets. In the Old Testament, the meteorological phenomenon of cloud has always been associated with the presence and glory of God, and no less so than at the ascension of Jesus. From that moment onward future appearances of Jesus to Stephen at his stoning, to Paul on the Damascus Road and to John on the island of Patmos, were of the Christ exalted to the right hand of the Father and resplendent in glorious light.

Jesus *last* words to the disciples (now called apostles) were for them to *wait* in Jerusalem. Then, when they had received God's power to be his witnesses, they would move out progressively beginning in Jerusalem, through all Judea and Samaria and to the ends of the earth.

It could be argued that the apostles were pre-emptive in the first decision they took whilst waiting for the promised power from on high. Peter, using two Davidic psalms (69.25; 109.8) reasoned that they should choose one from among their number to replace Judas Iscariot, who had betrayed Jesus. The criterion he established for making a shortlist was that this person had to be one who had been a witness to the Resurrection. As a result, Matthias was chosen and added to the eleven apostles. I mentioned that this may have been a pre-emptive decision on the part of the apostles, because Matthias is *never spoken of* again. But in the not too distant future, after the death of Stephen, the risen Christ appeared to Saul of Tarsus, a complete outsider, yet *divinely chosen* for apostolic duties. This particular individual was to become known as the apostle Paul, who did and wrote much on behalf of the gospel, and of whom a *great deal* has been said and written.

The apostles' message *(kerygma)*

The original eleven were right, however, in one important respect: the absolute test of an apostle was to have witnessed the resurrection of Jesus Christ, and is a clear indication that they themselves saw him after his resurrection. The Greek word, *Apostolos,* means literally 'one who is sent'. This practice is seen for the first time in Acts 13. 1-3, when the church in Antioch, under the guidance of the Holy Spirit, set apart Barnabas and Saul for the work to which the Lord had called them: "So after they had fasted and prayed, they placed their hands on them and sent them off."

The clear message preached by Peter on the Day of Pentecost was that Jesus had been raised from the dead by the mighty hand of God. This act of proclamation, or *kerygma* from the Greek language, carried the eye-witness authority of one to whom Jesus had appeared on numerous occasions during the previous weeks. The authority of Peter's preaching is seen in the response of the crowd, which was 'cut to the heart' and brought to repentance and faith that same day (Acts 2.37-41). The people responded in this way because they were fully aware of their part in the death of the Messiah. Rowan Williams puts it succinctly but with devastating force:

> This is not only an audience which knows about Jesus, an audience that has been a spectator of *ta peri Iesou tou Nazarenou,* 'the things concerning Jesus the Nazarene' (Luke 24.19). It is not a neutral audience, and it is not an innocent audience. In this event of the preaching of Jesus risen, there are no 'uninvolved by-standers'. For Luke, the apostles speak to an audience of

participants, an audience with blood on its hands. The proclaiming of Jesus crucified and risen is not a matter of giving information; the rhetoric of this preaching assumes that the hearers already belong in the story, that they are *agents,* that 'the things concerning Jesus' have concerned and will concern them. *(Resurrection,* Interpreting the Easter Gospel, pp. 1-2).

If the crowd or any who were part of the gathering that day had wished to disagree with Peter, they were at liberty to do so. And he challenged them to do so: "Men of Israel, listen to this: Jesus of Nazareth was a man accredited by God to you by miracles, wonders and signs, which God did among you through him, as you yourselves know." (Acts 2.22). But as we know, they did not contest the accusation. This message of Christ crucified and risen is a constant of the apostolic preaching (a message repeated almost word for word by Peter and the other apostles, when called to answer to the Jewish Sanhedrin after Pentecost (Acts 5.29-32); a message later taken up by the apostle Paul. The Resurrection was also central to Peter's message to the crowd, after the healing of the crippled man at the Temple's Beautiful Gate. "You killed the author of life, but God raised him from the dead. We are witnesses of this." (Acts 3.15). The historical record of this occasion (preserved by Luke), is informative of the 'where', 'when' and 'why'? regarding Peter's declaration. It was made in a specific place (the Temple Gate called Beautiful), at a specific time (three in the afternoon), and in connection with a specific circumstance (the healing of a man crippled from birth). The apostolic teaching, which the church follows to this day, is grounded in history from start to finish.

The meeting between Paul and the philosophers at the Areopagus was occasioned precisely because of his preaching about the Resurrection. This particular group of Athenians were characteristically curious to hear about new ideas and teaching. However, the notion of a bodily resurrection ran counter to their belief in the immortality of the soul, outside of the body. But this was the focus of his message: "For he (God) has set a day when he will judge the world with justice by the man he has appointed. He has given proof of this to all men by raising him from the dead." (Acts 17.31). His hearers at the Council gave him a mixed reception; some sneered, but some believed, including Dionysius, a member of the Areopagus, also a woman named Damaris (17.34). Luke, by giving the names of two of Paul's hearers, was open to be challenged by any individual or group who might dispute the accuracy of his statement regarding this encounter. This is similar to his narrative concerning Peter's preaching on the Day of Pentecost, where, at the end of his sermon about God raising Jesus from the dead, Peter says, "as you yourselves know." (Acts 2.22). As a historian, Luke was not afraid to use this technique, and at the same time it serves to reinforce the historicity of *all* that he relates, both in the book of Acts and the third Gospel. We may, therefore, safely conclude that both Peter and Paul preached that Jesus Christ rose from the dead by the power of God. This also begs the question, *why* did the apostles do this? From what we know of both Peter and Paul, neither of them would have been found preaching this sort of message, unless they knew it was true.

Steep learning curve

The church would soon have to face some difficult questions regarding its future direction and composition. An incident on a roof top in Joppa (Chapter 10) about what was acceptable or not acceptable to God came as a complete surprise to Peter. In the form of a vision during the midday siesta, he was presented with a situation, which to him was unthinkable: to eat meat considered by the Jews to be unclean. This was, of course, how they felt about the Gentiles. The mystery of the church in Paul's later teaching was exactly this, that the new community founded by Jesus Christ was to be inclusive of every race, colour and nationality. The concept of a church of all nations was built into the Great Commission, 'Go into all the world'. As in the Old Testament, God's self-revelation that he was the only God was *progressive*. It wasn't given all at once.

In the New Testament it is the same. Step by step he revealed his purposes to his people for a church of Jews and Gentiles, slave and free, where differences disappeared and *all* peoples became one in Christ Jesus.

The story of Cornelius (Chapter 10) is how this was drawn into sharp focus in the life of a specific individual and his family. Peter's dream and the visit to Peter by messengers sent by Cornelius were timed perfectly. On arriving at the house of Cornelius and witnessing the giving of the Holy Spirit to this family, Peter was assured that they, too, were part of God's family. How could it be otherwise? The gift of the Holy Spirit, as we already know, was *conditional* on the Ascension, which, in turn, *depended on* the Resurrection. In all these events, separately and sequentially, we are able to see the outworking of God's purposes on the stage of human history.

Clearly differences prevailed among the Jewish members of the church in Jerusalem over the situation regarding the Gentiles in Antioch and Asia Minor (Chapter 11). Peter was initially criticised for going in among them and eating with them (vv. 2-3). Upon hearing about his vision in Joppa and his experience at Caesarea, in the house of Cornelius, they all agreed that it was God's will that the Gentiles should be accepted on equal term with the Jewish believers. The resolution to this matter was given at the first council of the whole church, held in Jerusalem and chaired by James, the brother of Jesus (Chapter 15). After considerable discussion, the assembly was addressed by Peter, followed by Barnabas and Paul. When they had finished speaking James brought the proceedings to a close with the recommendation that the Gentile believers should be exempted from the Jewish ritual of circumcision, but abstain from certain meats and sexual immorality. After the Council, representatives of the Jerusalem church were sent with Paul and Barnabas to the churches in Antioch, Syria and Cilicia with a letter confirming the decision taken at the Council. This was done in the name of Jesus Christ, in whose risen life the church was growing in numbers on a daily basis, and towards a deeper understanding of God's sovereign purposes. The dynamics of the young church are sufficient evidence that for the believers this was a living faith in demonstration of the leading and power of the Holy Spirit: "It seemed good to the Holy Spirit and to us…" (Acts 15.28).

Stopped in his tracks

A further steep learning curve for the apostles in Jerusalem and the believers elsewhere was the conversion of Saul of Tarsus. They were still coming to terms with the dynamic operation of the Holy Spirit following the resurrection and ascension of Jesus. Saul's conversion is further evidence that Jesus rose from the dead, as we shall explain. The first to face this head on was Ananias, a disciple living in Damascus. Following Saul's dramatic experience on the road to Damascus, he was taken into the city, blinded and disorientated. Ananias was then entrusted with the task of going to the house where Saul was staying and to place his hands on him and restore the sight of this persecutor of the church. The act of restoring this man's sight was performed in the name of the *Lord* Jesus. It is significant that Saul was made aware of this before the act was performed. We can be confident that Saul received his sight because he now believed and this is confirmed insofar as he was immediately baptised and remained for several days with the disciples in Damascus, and even began preaching in the synagogues that Jesus was the Christ (the Jewish Messiah), putting his own life in considerable danger, to the point that he had to secretly escape the city (see Acts 9.23-25).

Jesus: Dead or Alive?

The appearance of Jesus to Saul of Tarsus on the road to Damascus was unlike his appearances to the disciples in Jerusalem and Galilee. He could be heard, but not seen in physical form. His presence was felt, but not comprehended by those who witnessed this supernatural event. The event itself might have been dismissed, if it had not been witnessed by others who were there. Not only is the event itself significant, but the outcome for Saul and those who had heard of his reputation as a persecutor of the church, is historically incontrovertible. There can be no more straight-forward explanation for the transformation that Saul experienced, other than that this was as real as anything in his life before or after. There was a blinding light and a voice, seen and heard with Saul's physical eyes and ears and of those who were travelling with him, though Jesus they did not see. Even though Jesus was not seen, he made himself known to Saul and of this Saul had no doubt, not then or at any time thereafter. Visions, to be proven, have to be supported and explained by real-life confirmations and consequences. In the example of Peter's vision, Cornelius was the solid evidence upon which this vision was grounded. In the case of Saul of Tarsus, it was the life and work of Paul the apostle, following a remarkable encounter with the risen Christ.

Chapter Seven

In the teaching of Paul

The message of Paul is grounded in his first-hand experience of the risen Christ. He had obtained letters from the religious authorities in Jerusalem, and was in pursuit of those who belonged to the new movement known as 'The Way' and attached to the synagogues in Damascus. As we have seen in the previous chapter of this book, on the journey to that city the risen Christ appeared to him in blinding and unapproachable light, brighter than the sun, and changed him forever. His undivided attention had been given to eradicating this new movement. Saul, as he was known before his conversion, was also present at the stoning of the first Christian martyr, Stephen. Paul experienced a complete turnaround from persecutor of the church to ambassador of Jesus Christ. He, himself, explains his *life and ambition* before and after his encounter with the risen Christ in his letter to the church at Philippi, a Roman colony on the European mainland. He sums up his *new life in Christ* in an earlier letter to the churches in Galatia, part of modern-day Turkey. His *teaching about the Resurrection* is found in his first letter to the church in Corinth, a busy cosmopolitan city of ancient Greece.

The main points of Paul's teaching are as follows:
1. Christ died for our sins according to the Scriptures

(Psalm 22.1; Isaiah 53). 2. He was buried and raised on the third day, according to the Scriptures (Psalm 16.9-10; Jonah 1.17; cf. Matthew 12.40). 3. Christ appeared to Peter and then to the Twelve. Paul's account that Jesus appeared to Peter first corroborates the testimony of the group in Jerusalem on the first Easter Sunday. As we have already seen, the two disciples who hurriedly returned to Jerusalem from Emmaus with the story of their meeting with Jesus along the way and in their home, were greeted with the affirmation 'He is indeed risen and has appeared to Peter'. 4. After that, says Paul, he appeared to more than five hundred of his followers at a single moment in time. Most were still living at the time Paul wrote these words (so they could corroborate his testimony). 5. Jesus then appeared to James, and then to all the apostles. 6. Finally, he appeared to Paul (Saul as he was then known) the arch-persecutor of the followers of Jesus. Paul considers the facts of the Resurrection to be 'of first importance', and upon which rests our faith and the proclamation of the gospel.

The record of the resurrection appearances to which Paul refers, omits the appearance of Jesus to the women and the two disciples on the road to Emmaus. He also places Jesus' appearance to James after his appearance to five hundred of his followers at one time. The omission of the women (as we have already noted) may have to do with the prevailing Jewish culture (at that time), regarding the testimony of women, rather than a lapse of historical accuracy. James, however, is placed after the appearance to the five-hundred. This naturally brings into question the hypothesis put forward earlier that James could have been the first to see Jesus after his resurrection. Also, who was the young man in the tomb, who (according to the Gospel of Mark) greeted the women when they arrived at first light? He might have been an angel, as angels mostly appear in the Bible in human form. Might *he* have been the first person to witness the Resurrection? Whatever the answer to these questions, we are concerned with objective truth, so will do no more than mention these finer points, as significant as they *may prove to be* for knowing the whole story.

Evidence from earliest times

Returning to the statement about the resurrection appearances of Jesus, Paul informs the church in Corinth that, at some point in time, he had received this statement of early Christian belief. Therefore, he did not write it except, of course, the final affirmation concerning his personal encounter with the risen Lord, on the road to Damascus. This credal statement, was therefore written before Paul wrote his first letter to the Corinthian church. Lee Strobel, in his book, *The Case for Christ,* records the following remarks by Gary Habermas: "We know that Paul wrote 1 Corinthians between AD 55 and AD 57. He indicates in 1 Corinthians 15.1-4 that he had already passed on this creed to the church at Corinth, which would mean it must predate his visit there in AD 51. Therefore, the creed was being used within twenty years of the Resurrection." (p. 310). However, Habermas continues that it could well be much earlier, and that Paul received it from the church in Damascus, or from Peter or James on the occasion of his visit to Jerusalem, which would place it at around two to eight years after the Resurrection. If this creed was as early as Habermas claims, then the oral traditions are even earlier, dating back to the events themselves. The idea that the story of the Resurrection originated in the late first century church is brought into question, when we consider the prominence of the women in the *written* account. They would almost certainly have been omitted by the pen of the writer, as they were from the creed to which Paul refers, unless their presence and part in the story is entirely factual, and they had actually witnessed the empty tomb and seen the risen Lord.

Affirming the Resurrection

The apostle Paul had a great intellect and has contributed on a grand scale to our Christian understanding of God. But it was always from the heart that he spoke of the risen Jesus. He knew with his heart as well as his mind that Jesus rose from the dead. The background to this conviction has already been stated. It was grounded in a dramatic personal encounter with Jesus whilst in pursuit of the followers of 'The Way', as the church was known at the beginning of its history. Paul's conviction that Jesus had overcome death and the grave is evident also in his absolute certainty about the corporal resurrection of those who believe in Christ. This is summed up in his words to the church at Corinth: "Thanks be to God who gives us the victory through our Lord Jesus Christ." (1 Corinthians 15.57).

In defence of his apostleship and his right to be called an apostle, Paul declares that he had seen the risen Lord. "Have I not seen Jesus our Lord?" (1 Corinthians

9.1). My understanding of an apostle is that it is one who *witnessed* the resurrection, or at least was a companion of those who had done so. The word is used much more loosely today, though the qualification would still depend on adherence to the original meaning of the Greek word *Apostolos*, 'one who is sent'. However, Paul clearly underlines the importance of having witnessed the resurrection of Jesus, from which he claims the title for himself and also the authority that goes with it.

But it is not only to the church at Corinth that Paul emphatically asserts that Jesus rose from the dead; neither solely in defence of his right to be called an apostle. To the church in Rome, he says: "Christ Jesus, who died – more than that, who was raised to life – is at the right hand of God and is also interceding for us" (Romans 8.34); again to the Corinthian church: "But Christ has indeed been raised from the dead, the first-fruits of those who have fallen asleep" (1 Corinthians 15.20); "And he died for all, that those who live should no longer live for themselves, but for him who died for them and was raised again" (2 Corinthians 5.15); to the church at Ephesus: "and his incomparably great power... which he exerted in Christ when he raised him from the dead and seated him at his right hand..." (Ephesians 1.20); and to the Christians in Philippi: "I want to know Christ and the power of his resurrection" (Philippians 3.10). It was clearly no passing phase, but a deep-seated and unswerving conviction of both heart and mind. It is worth remembering the words of Josephus about the persistence of the church and the *ongoing* witness of the Christians a whole generation later.

This is also documented in his renowned *Antiquities of Jewish History,* Book 18.3.3.

A body fit for heaven

Paul also writes to the Christians in Corinth about the resurrection body. He explains in graphic terms that as the 'first-fruits' of those who have fallen asleep, Jesus is the guarantor that those who follow him will rise with him and obtain the glorious body of the resurrection. This is a body like his resurrection body, *bearing the marks* of an earthly body, but *free from the limitations* of our earthly bodies. It will be an incorruptible body, free from disease and decay and fit for its role in heaven (1 Corinthians 15.35-55). The body which Jesus assumed after the Resurrection was different from the body he had before. In his resurrection body he was able to move in an instant from one place to another and pass through locked doors. Of relevance here is earlier reference to the stone which had been rolled away from the entrance to the tomb. This was not so that he could leave the tomb, but, rather, that others could enter and see inside. And, as the first-fruits of those that sleep, Jesus post-resurrection body is a prototype of the kind with which we will be clothed at his coming in glory.

In the same way that the risen Christ was recognisable to those who knew him, so will it be for those who have died, believing in his power to raise them also from the dead. The fact that Jesus was not instantly recognised by the disciples may be down to two post-resurrection factors: firstly, the disciples simply did not expect that Jesus would rise again; secondly, there was a perceptible change in his appearance, though the marks of the cross were still visible (the definitive confirmation that it was Jesus). Paul describes the resurrection body of those who sleep, believing in him, in glorious terms: "So will it be with the resurrection of the dead. The body that is sown is perishable, it is raised imperishable; it is sown in dishonour, it is raised in glory; it is sown in weakness, it is raised in power; it is sown a natural body, it is raised a spiritual body." (1 Corinthians 15.42-44). The resurrection of Jesus is not only something to cheer about (as happening to someone else), it is something to celebrate (as happening to us)!

Life in Christ in the here and now

Paul is not only concerned with the future life in heaven. He is very clear about the new life in the present world: "And if the Spirit of him who raised Jesus from the dead is living in you, he who raised Christ from the dead will also give life to your mortal bodies through his Spirit, who lives in you." (Romans 8.11). For Paul, all faith must be based on the assumption that Christ was raised from the dead (1 Corinthians 15.17). A. M. Hunter, in his book, *The Gospel According to St. Paul*, offers the following critical evaluation of Christian faith today as seen through the eyes of the apostle Paul:

> There are still those among us who imagine that the Christian life is a kind of harking-back to the first century in the endeavour to follow Christ as the

first disciples did in Galilee. They need
to learn from Paul that the essence of
being a Christian lies in fellowship with
a *contemporary* Christ, a Christ no
longer cramped and confined as in "the
days of his flesh" but "let loose in the
world", by the Resurrection and the
coming of the Spirit, to be a ubiquitous
and universal Saviour. (p. 101).

This interpretation of Paul's thinking is backed up
by the words of Jesus to the women returning from the
empty tomb: "Do not be afraid. Go and tell my brothers to
go to Galilee; there they will see me." (Matthew 28.10).
Without attempting to stretch these words beyond their
original meaning, it is within the scope of biblical
exposition to understand that they are inclusive of all those
who would follow him *today* – wherever *their* Galilee may
be. The reality of Easter faith is exactly this. The
experience of the risen Christ is extended not only to those
who saw with their *physical eyes* and believed (like
Thomas on seeing the Lord's wounded hands and side), but
especially to those who (like John on entering the empty
tomb) have seen with the *eyes of faith*. It is among these
that *we* stand before Christ today.

There has been considerable discussion about the
Jesus of history. How far can we know him, or know *about*
him, through the stories surrounding his life and ministry?
Scholars like Rudolf Bultmann and his followers and also
the American New Testament researcher, Bart Ehrman,
would go to great lengths to bring into question the

historical context of the Gospel narrative about Jesus of Nazareth, reducing it to mythological storytelling on the part of the primitive church. They would not go as far as to say that Jesus never existed, rather their doubts have to do with the claims made about him by his followers. It is our endeavour to show in the next chapter of this book, that there is a direct link between us and the historical Jesus, through the unbroken chain of witness from the apostles through successive generations down to our own. We shall also look into the reason why this chain of witness has remained unbroken for two thousand years.

If we look closely at John's Gospel, we will see that it is interpretive of the synoptic tradition, which largely tells the story as it unfolded in time and space. John is the vital link between the 'then' and 'now', that is, the primitive message and the living Christ who Paul encountered so unexpectedly, and in such dramatic fashion, on the Damascus Road. Taken at face value, the synoptic gospels convey to us the *historical* dimension of faith; what happened, when and where. John, however, brings us the *theological* dimension, though it would be wrong to think that John's Gospel is not to be trusted as an historical account of the life of Jesus. Rather, it is the springboard from the Jesus of history to the Christ of personal reflective faith, direct encounter and immediate experience. This is exactly where Paul takes up the role of ambassador of Jesus Christ "as though God were making his appeal through us." (2 Corinthians 5.20). There is no mistake that he considers himself to be the representative of the *living God* and his Christ.

Jesus: Dead or Alive?

The historical Jesus, as the first disciples knew him (in a localised Galilean context, during a period of three years), is now the universal Christ of eternity. Through the gift of his Spirit, we are able to know him and fellowship with him in our own particular time and space. This is also for the present time. That is, as Paul says, "until we see (him) face to face." (1Corinthians 13.12). Though Paul does not mention exactly who we shall see 'face to face', "Christ was so central to Paul's thinking that there is no real doubt about that" (Leon Morris, *The First Epistle of Paul to the Corinthians,* p. 188). Paul, it is true, never knew Jesus in the way that the twelve disciples knew him, or witnessed his life from his baptism to his resurrection, the criteria established for being part of that exclusive and elite group. Yet he could say, without reservation, "Christ lives in me." (Galatians 2.20).

Paul's formidable contribution to Christian thought, his impact on the world and his considerable ability to cause upheaval by preaching Christ crucified and risen, wherever he went, were unparalleled in the early church. It may seem strange to us that he did not attempt to overturn the social and cultural norms of his day, regarding the role of women and the place of slavery in society, but he was adamant that Jesus was, *after all,* the promised Jewish Messiah, whose sphere of authority was the whole world and all time. The thrust of Paul's preaching was this: wherever we happen to be, in whatever situation of life, at whatever moment in history, we are able to enjoy and be transformed by the life-changing presence of Christ. He is always our *contemporary.* This, as we have seen from his

In the teaching of Paul

own testimony, is Paul's *constant theme* and the *clear meaning* of the Resurrection.

PART THREE

Appealing to the evidence

Chapter Eight

The testimony of the church

The church believed that Jesus was *Lord*, by virtue of his resurrection from the dead. It was *after* the Resurrection that Jesus was addressed as Lord by his followers. Before the Resurrection, the disciples addressed him as 'Master', 'Teacher' or 'Rabbi'. We find this way of addressing Jesus to be used throughout the Gospel narratives until the Resurrection. There is one exception to this and it comes from the lips of Mary Magdalene at the garden tomb, when Jesus first appeared to her. It was quite natural that she should address Jesus in the way she always had done (John 20.16). When she reached the disciples with the news that she had seen him and told them what he had said to her, she no longer refers to him as 'Rabbi': "I have seen the Lord!", she exclaims (John 20.18). This is true also of John, who recognising Jesus on the shoreline of Galilee, called to the other disciples in the boat. 'It is the Lord!' (John 21.7). This translated into the credal statements of the early Church, for example: "If you confess with your mouth, 'Jesus is Lord,' and believe in your heart that God raised him from the dead, you will be saved." (Romans 10.9). The confession as to Jesus status arises out of the conviction that God raised him from the dead. This marks a change in the relationship of Jesus to his followers. He is now not only one who imparts learning, but also life at a new level of meaning. Jesus is now the focus of their *worship,* a point illustrated by the women who, returning from the empty tomb, *clasp his feet* (in the eastern world, a token of homage and adoration) as he greets them along the way (Matthew 28.9). This new relationship permeates the life of the church and is central to its worship and witness in the world. If the disciples had not believed that Jesus had risen from the dead, they would, in their innermost psyche, have continued to think of him as they always had done, as a beloved teacher, known affectionately to them as 'Master'. There is no particular reason, other than the fact of the Resurrection, that accounts for this new way of addressing Jesus or for elevating his person to the status of deity, as implied by the title 'Lord'. And Paul states quite clearly that this was indeed the reason: "...who as to his human nature was a descendant of David, and who through the Spirit of holiness was declared with power to be the Son of God, by his resurrection from the dead: Jesus Christ our Lord." (Romans 1.3-4). Paul had undergone a dramatic change of heart, and this was not, according to him, by the testimony of others, not even the eyewitnesses, but as he, himself, says, when writing to the churches in Galatia: "I want you to know, brothers, that the gospel I preached is not something that man made up. I did not receive it from any man, nor was I taught it; rather, I received it by revelation from Jesus Christ." (Galatians 1.11-12). He then goes on to describe his career (life's mission) before his encounter with Christ, and his subsequent 180° turnabout (Greek *metanoia).* This is picked up in his letter to the church at Philippi: "I press on to take hold of that for which Christ took hold of me." (Philippians 3.12). These statements are the result of, and consistent with, his life-changing experience of meeting the risen Christ. Paul's conversion on the Damascus Road is the enabling of hope within successive generations that the Jesus of history is not locked into the past, forever more distant from us, but our living contemporary and the contemporary of future generations.

The Resurrection was a powerful event that resulted in a powerful message. On a single day, the Day of Pentecost, about three thousand new believers were added to their number. The message changed the way of life of those who believed it to be true. On that remarkable day, the Holy Spirit did two things: he gave the gift of *speech* to the apostles, and to those who heard he gave the gift of *hearing*, which enabled the hearers to *connect* with the burning issues of the message as it was delivered. They met together in the Temple on a daily basis and shared in the breaking of bread every Sunday. They gave testimony to their faith in Jesus and performed miracles in his name. "And the Lord added to their number daily those who were being saved." (Acts 2.47). The leaders of the church defied the religious authorities at great personal risk. They were flogged, but continued preaching and healing the sick in the name of Jesus. One of their number, Stephen, was stoned to death for preaching the name of Jesus in defiance of the Jewish authorities. James, the brother of John, was also martyred at the capriciousness of King Herod Agrippa.

The first Christians not only witnessed the Resurrection they witnessed to it (that is, they *lived* it out in their daily lives, and they also *died* for it). The existence of the church can only be reasonably explained as a sequel to this historical event. The earliest Christian community was made up of first-hand witnesses, whose lives had been transformed and whose changed behaviour can only be explained in the light of the Resurrection. When the apostles chose a successor to Judas Iscariot, the criterion was that that person should have witnessed the Resurrection, as they themselves had. For the founding members of the church, the heart of their life and message was the unswerving conviction that, somehow, he who was dead is now alive for evermore (Revelation 1.18).

Unbroken chain

Down the centuries, the church that Christ had in mind to build has been comprised of believers who have received the message from a succession of other believers. That is those who passed the message on, starting with the original eye-witnesses. As an illustration of this, we can go back to John, an immediate disciple of Jesus, and his disciple, Polycarp, bishop of Smyrna, and his disciple, Irenaeus, bishop of Lyon, and continue this process successively throughout the centuries to the present day. There is an unbroken historic chain, which leads back to that first Easter Sunday.

Working backwards, Irenaeus (c. 130-202 AD) mentions Papias (c. 60-163 AD) who wrote down the oral traditions which he heard from John the Elder concerning the apostles, including the apostle John. Papias was a hearer of John the Elder and a companion of Polycarp. And we know that Polycarp was a disciple of John the apostle, who was an immediate disciple of Jesus Christ. Although we cannot be sure, it is possible that the apostle John was also known as 'John the Elder' at that time, and so these two could be one and the same person (see the opening words of 2 and 3 John verse 1). The following is from Eusebius, bishop of Caesarea (c. 260-340 AD), in his *Ecclesiastical History,* Book III: "So, indeed, says Irenaeus: Nevertheless Papias himself, in the preface to his discourses, makes it plain that he was in no sense a hearer and eye-witness of the holy apostles; but tells us, by the language he uses, that he had received the things pertaining to the faith from those who were their pupils." (*A New Eusebius*, p. 50). The earliest written documents are therefore based on oral traditions handed down from the apostles and their immediate disciples and so have their origin in the time of the apostles and Jesus, himself. To give due emphasis to this important point, two of the above mentioned, Polycarp and Papias, were of the generation of witnesses immediately following the apostles, themselves. Polycarp, as we have already seen, was a direct disciple of the apostle John. These second-generation witnesses of Jesus Christ are known in church history as the 'Apostolic Fathers'.

As for the church, yesterday and today, it exists solely in consequence of the Resurrection, and is the living evidence in every age that Jesus was raised from the dead on the third day following his crucifixion. The church is his earthly body joined to his glorious, risen life. The origin of the church (and that of its message) is the historic event of the Resurrection, which is also the raison d'être of its mission. Without the Resurrection, there is simply no story to tell; without the risen Christ, the church and its message would have long since disappeared and been forgotten in the mists of time. A wise and learned member of the Jewish Sanhedrin, Gamaliel (who taught Saul of Tarsus in matters of Jewish law) was right when he advised the Council to allow the passage of time to tell whether or not this new religious movement was from God. If it was not, he said, it would come to nothing, and gives examples of other new movements that ended after their leaders were killed (Acts 5.38-39). To further illustrate this point, a century after Gamaliel, in AD 132, Simon Bar Kochba, a self-declared messiah and his followers were successful in bringing about not only their own destruction, but the destruction of the entire city of Jerusalem by the hand of the Emperor Hadrian and six Roman legions (see Merrill C. Tenney, *New Testament Times,* p. 348). This destruction was even greater than in AD 70 under Titus, and what remained of the Jewish state was finally gone.

An efficient and less costly way to destroy a movement or organisation, is to allow this to happen from within; that is, to leave it to implode of its own accord. The Roman emperor, Claudius, had this idea with regard to the church. He decided not to attack it, but rather let it self-destruct by what he perceived to be internal rivalry for positions of leadership. The anticipated implosion did not happen. No more than when the church endured persecution, local, universal, sporadic or official was he able to extinguish the flame or deter its progress. Gamaliel was not only wise in the way he advised the Jewish Sanhedrin; he was also right in predicting the outcome. In retrospect, this would seem to confirm the divinely inspired motivation and tenacity, which has guaranteed the survival of the church to the present day. A long line of witnesses (Greek *martyrion)*, beginning with the apostles, has continued to reach out through successive generations of believers, to the point of touching our present-day lives with the reality of the risen Christ. We have it here: "My prayer is not for them alone. I pray also for those who will believe in me through their message." (John 17.20). This progression was envisaged by Jesus, who is also its guarantor.

All authority

Jesus had been given all authority in heaven and on earth (Matthew 28.18), and with this authority he endowed his disciples for their future work. The authority which Jesus received from the Father is the authority by which the church is sent out to witness to the Resurrection in every age. "As the Father sent me, so I send you." There is an explicit connection between this Johannine text and the Matthean version of the Great Commission, "Go, therefore, and make disciples of all nations..." the *authority* the church has received is from the risen Christ, exalted to the right hand of God, and the *command* he gives is to go to all nations. Though we are subject to the world's authorities, which themselves have been established by God (Romans 13), his authority is over all in heaven and on earth. Jesus is vindicated by virtue of the Resurrection. He spent forty days giving adequate proofs of this, and of which at least five hundred people were witnesses. Not just the eleven, but five hundred others, though some doubted initially. But those who saw him, knew for certain that it was Jesus. People such as Thomas (John 20), the seven on a fishing trip on the Sea of Galilee (John 21), and those who went out to meet him on the mountain, also in Galilee (Matthew 28). This was not because they were experiencing hallucinations, but because he had told the women returning from the empty tomb: "Go and tell my brothers to go to Galilee; there they will see me." For so many different people to see Jesus either in small or large groups is sufficient reason to disavow the hallucination theory. Hallucinations are the experience of individuals and not a phenomenon witnessed by others.

For those who consider the appearances of Jesus to be mere hallucinations, the following observation by James Denney is apposite:

> There is no such thing in the New Testament as an appearance of the Risen Saviour in which he merely appears. He is always represented as entering into relation to those who see him in ways other than by a flash upon the inner or the outer eye. He establishes other communications between himself and his own besides those which can be characterised in this way. He not only appeared to them, but spoke to them. He not only appeared to them, but taught them, and in particular gave them a commission in which the

The testimony of the church

meaning of his own life and work, and their calling as connected with it, are finally declared. In every known form of the evangelic tradition such a charge, or instruction, or commission, is found on the lips of Jesus after the resurrection. *The Death of Christ,* (p. 44).

It is interesting to note in the context of the above, that when Mary Magdalene met Jesus at the garden tomb, she recognised him by his voice, at the moment when he called her by name: "Jesus said to her, '*Mary.*' " (John 20.16).

Ring of truth

The Gospel record concerning the life and ministry of Jesus has not always been taken at face value. The German Lutheran scholar, Rudolf Bultmann, was convinced that the *stories surrounding Jesus* were shrouded in ancient myth, obscuring our ability to discover what Jesus was really like and what he actually said and, more importantly, did, especially in respect of the miracle stories. It is precisely the *historical situations* into which the sayings of Jesus have been *inserted*, that have given rise to doubt and suspicion, beginning with Albert Schweitzer's *quest of the historical Jesus*. Of particular interest here, is Bultmann's negation of the Resurrection as a *historical and physical event*. Bultmann argues that we cannot know the historical Jesus from *the narratives* describing his life and ministry

131

on earth. These stories, he claims, have little or no historical value. The assumption is that the stories were simply the product of the late first-century church's own projected thinking about Jesus, rather than a precise record of his personal activity. That said, there would appear to be a degree of supposition and assumption behind this particular reading of the Gospels. If the stories had been *invented* for the purpose of giving a historical and geographical context to the church's teaching about Jesus, one might have expected the different writers to exercise greater diligence in matters of detail, as well as substance (even to the point of collusion), for it is here (in relation to the *differences* between the accounts), that much doubt has arisen.

It is natural that traditions like 'Q' to which Matthew and Luke turned, and the oral accounts which Papias drew on, should have focussed on *what Jesus said*, rather than *when and where* it was said. The fact that there *are* discrepancies between one story and another does give a certain *ring of truth* to them. This is because the stories were handed down as stories always are; by word of mouth. Inevitably, in the normal way, variations will have crept in. But these do not detract from the bigger picture, or the core agreement regarding the life setting, *sitz im leben*, of Jesus and his ministry. The different records are entirely consistent in this respect: Jesus chose *Galilee* as the main region of his preaching and teaching ministry (except for trips to Jerusalem, in order to take part in the principal religious festivals); it was in *Galilee* that Jesus chose his first disciples, who left their day to day work to follow him; Jesus chose, as the base for his itinerant ministry, Capernaum, a fishing village on *the north-west shore of the Sea of Galilee.* The Galilean ministry was at the heart of his life on earth; on this point, all are agreed.

It is the extraordinary claim that Jesus rose from the dead that is subject to special scrutiny and objection. In an attempt to cast *doubt* on the historical validity of these appearances, critics have examined the *detail* in the narratives and have reached the conclusion that there are notable discrepancies between one account and another. The same depth of analysis has also been undertaken in this book, but strangely the detail points us in the *opposite* direction.

Evidence supporting the *authenticity* of the resurrection narratives is given by the evangelical scholar, Leon Morris, who draws attention to scenes in the Fourth Gospel, which he considers to be indicative of nothing less than genuine eyewitness testimony. Firstly, the scene at the tomb. The details are given by the author of this Gospel, who says that the younger disciple arrived first. We are then told of this disciple's initial hesitation to go inside the tomb, but that *when he did enter, he believed.* Secondly, the prominence given to Thomas, who was not a conspicuous member of the band of disciples. However, *his slowness to believe is placed centre stage* on the Sunday after the Resurrection. Thirdly, regarding the fishing trip on the Sea of Galilee. We are told that Peter *put on his outer garment before plunging into the sea,* so as to reach the shore (where Jesus was waiting) in the shortest possible time. This act of 'getting dressed' would be an unusual thing for someone to do before going for a swim in the sea. Morris argues that the inclusion of these details would only be worth reporting *if they had actually happened.* These, otherwise, minor details draw us inexorably towards an authentic eyewitness account (see *Studies in the Fourth Gospel*, pp. 203-206).

Bultmann, whose views I have already mentioned, may have had a surprising *change of mind* at the close of his life. At his funeral service, and with his approval, the following *double* affirmation of the Resurrection was included among the readings: "And if the Spirit of him who *raised Jesus from the* dead is living in you, he who *raised Christ from the dead* will also give life to your mortal bodies through his Spirit, who lives in you." (Romans 8.11). This along with the other readings from Scripture were allowed to stand alone, without further commentary or qualification.

The narratives in the synoptic gospels are based on *four different sources,* as I shall explain: firstly, 'Q' (an unidentified collection of Jesus' sayings, material which is common to Matthew and Luke, but not found in Mark); secondly, material which is original to Mark; thirdly, material exclusive to Matthew, and fourthly, material unique to Luke. We know that Matthew and Luke relied on Mark for most of their material, but not all of it. We acknowledge, therefore, that there are several traditions from which the Gospel records have been drawn. If these three Gospels were identical in presentation and content, some kind of collusion would have been suspected and used as an argument against their authenticity. As it is, there are divergencies, and it is these divergencies that have been cited to contest the trustworthiness of the accounts *received and handed down* by the early church.

The testimony of the church

The plain truth is that whilst there is evidence of *dependence* on Mark and Q by Matthew and Luke, there is no evidence of *collusion*; there are clearly divergencies in the detail, but *total agreement in matters of substance*, most importantly, regarding the empty tomb and the appearances of Jesus, on numerous occasions, to different people, individually and in groups from two to five hundred, after his resurrection from the dead. In this respect, *all four Gospels are in complete agreement*.

The church continues to exist because the evidence for the Resurrection is given to be trustworthy and true. The embryonic church was called into existence two thousand years ago *to witness first-hand the victory of Jesus over death and the grave*: the instructions he gave to his disciples were clear and simple; "You shall be my witnesses." (Acts 1.8). Likewise, today, the church exists *to bear witness to its risen Lord*.

Symbols of resurrection power

The most important day in the life of the church is Easter Sunday. Every weekly act of worship is one of thanksgiving and celebration because of Easter Sunday. This is why the church meets for worship on that day. The transforming power of the Resurrection to make all things new, is still at work. The healing, forgiving, restoring power of Jesus in and through the church is the outward sign. Another sign is Christian baptism, an ordinance which signals admission into the church, but more significantly it represents new life through the death, burial and resurrection of Jesus. When new members are added to the church in this way, those individuals bear witness to this reality in their own lives. The church perpetuates this symbolic act in obedience to the command of Jesus, and because it believes in the reality behind this symbolic act. Symbols such as words and gestures are powerful as representing the realities they enshrine. The teaching of the apostles, which has been passed down through the centuries, is not about the apostles or about a great moral teacher. This, in itself, would not have been sufficient to enable the Christian faith to survive, let alone advance the mission of Christ on the world stage, in the way it has done, across nations and cultures. The central message of the church is not so much in the words it proclaims, but in the stories and realities behind those words. Its message is centred on the risen Christ and the evidence of transformed lives by the power of his resurrection.

Jewish beginnings

The church since the first century might not have been what Jesus had in mind, whatever exactly that was. Has the organised church become an aberration of the vision that Jesus had for it? Does it represent *his* vision for those whom he 'called out' to be his *ekklesia*? At a local level of Christian communities, serving the wider community on behalf of the risen Lord, the answer to the second question is undoubtedly 'yes'. The longevity of the Christian faith is rooted in the purpose of Jesus to *build* his church, against which no kind of opposition will ever prevail.

We have observed and drawn attention to the fact that the early Jerusalem church continued its links with the

Jewish tradition of temple worship. There was no clean break between the church in Jerusalem and the Jewish faith of old. Indeed, Jesus, as Messiah, was seen by the church to be the fulfilment, and not the end of the Jewish way of life. That was to come forty years later (as predicted by Jesus) with the fall of Jerusalem. The Jerusalem church was, in fact, initially, distinctly parochial, and it was not until the martyrdom of Stephen that it moved beyond its own 'four walls'. The next significant moment was the Jerusalem Council, which decided the terms on which non-Jewish members were to be incorporated into the church, together with the recognition that God's favour had been shown to them also.

On his missionary journeys, it is well known that Paul adopted the custom of preaching first in the synagogues, and it was only after opposition from the Jews that he moved to neutral ground (Acts 18.7;19.9) and set his sights on taking the gospel primarily to the Gentiles (Acts 18.6). It was probably not until after AD 70 with the destruction of Jerusalem and its temple that the Christian community became formally separated from its Jewish origins. Tacitus, however, gives the impression that for the Christians in Rome, this separation occurred some years before that date, possibly around the time of the expulsion of the Jews in the reign of the Emperor Claudius, AD 41-54. Luke also refers to this particular episode in Acts 18.1-2. This agreement between the records of a secular historian such as Tacitus and Luke's account, enables us to appraise the historical reliability of the book of Acts and, by extension, the Gospel of Luke.

Jesus: Dead or Alive?

He who makes things grow

Jesus commanded the disciples to make disciples among the nations, beginning in Jerusalem. It was only at the onset of persecution that, in a series of subsequent waves, it moved outwards towards its eventual goal, the capital of the ancient world – Rome. From the heart of Europe, the message was taken to the New World during the Age of Discovery in the 15th and 16th centuries. At that time the traffic was from the northern hemisphere to the southern, where today the church is growing faster than in any other part of the terrestrial globe. The epicentre of Christianity has moved from Jerusalem to Antioch; from Antioch to Asia Minor; from Asia Minor to Europe; from Europe to the New World. The last of these was in the name of colonisation, where unprepared cultures have been subjected to the religious values of those politically more powerful. In Europe, the might of medieval Catholicism ruled until the light of the Gospel shone through the Reformation. But this new movement was fragmented from the start, with different leaders and doctrines vying for influence from Germany (Luther) to Switzerland (Zwingli), to France (Calvin), and finally to England, through the sovereign's personal convenience. Today, in the southern hemisphere, charismatic leaders wrestle for control, and new churches appear on every street corner on a seemingly daily basis.

The testimony of the church is not always as unambiguous as it might be. Paul argued for a clearer message as far back as first-century Corinth: "What, after

138

all, is Apollos? And what is Paul? Only servants, through whom you came to believe – as the Lord has assigned to each his task. I planted the seed, Apollos watered it, but God made it grow. Neither he who plants nor he who waters is anything, but only God, who makes things grow." (1 Corinthians 3.5-7). This does not eulogise the church, but affirms that for all its faults, God is able to achieve his purposes *through* the church. Incredibly, as Paul infers, God uses *the church,* in order to bring others to a living faith in *the risen Lord.*

The church's witness has been mixed through the course of its history. It started off in that way, with a mixed bag of disciples During the first century, the church sometimes left much to be desired; the church in Corinth being a prime example of a church that fell short of the mark. However, the message the church is called to preach is not about the *church*, but about *Christ.* We do not invite people to come to church; we invite them to come to Christ. I remember Dr Barry White of Regents Park College, Oxford, speaking at a London church, saying exactly this. It has remained with me ever since; it has shaped the way I think about the church. When churches grow (and this is happening in many parts of the world today), this should not be the cause for self-congratulation, but rather a sign that people are still being drawn to Christ, not because of persuasive preaching (not even the apostle Paul succeeded in that *all* the time), or manipulative methods (though, unfortunately, these are sometimes used by preachers on the *periphery* of the church), but because the *one* who sows and the *one* who waters can still depend on the good services of the *One* who makes things grow.

Epilogue

Does it make any difference, whether or not we believe Jesus rose from the dead? To those who believe that he did, it is the greatest event in human history. For those who choose to *believe* otherwise, there are likely to remain many other questions concerning the life and ministry of Jesus, none more pressing than those concerning the miracle stories and his own miraculous birth, let alone the greatest miracle of them all – his resurrection.

My aim in this book has been to be at all times *objective*. Over the past two centuries there has been a great deal of discussion and argument regarding the basis upon which the events surrounding the life of Jesus have been tested as historically factual. Do the Gospel narratives meet the historiographical tests now generally considered necessary for establishing their reliability concerning Jesus of Nazareth? The recognised tests include the following: to what degree are the different writers relying on independent sources for their information? Are there internal contradictions within the different accounts? Is there historical evidence outside the Gospels for the existence of Jesus? I must confess that I did not consciously apply these tests as I went along, but only after concluding my examination of the evidence in detail. Only then did I apply the tests to see if my research would survive such critical scrutiny. To my delight and surprise, the reasons I had given for accepting the written traditions as they stand seem to have passed the latest historiographical tests, wherever they are relevant to the conclusions I have reached and the arguments upon which these conclusions are based. Furthermore, I sense that those who have raised objections to the historicity of the Resurrection have sometimes been selective in their observations and have not always faced the evidence full on. Whatever one's thoughts and opinions about the Resurrection, the starting point will be either acceptance or incredulity. There are occasions when minds have been changed, looking more closely into the story, or after experiencing a lightning bolt of revelation. Frank Morison and the apostle Paul, respectively, are examples of when this has happened. Perhaps the important thing is to have an *open mind*, because if we approach these matters with a closed mind, it is less likely we will discover the truth, but simply remain with our presuppositions. What is the *real* difference between 'I *believe* that such a thing happened' and 'I *cannot believe* that it happened'? Each of these statements is the result of intellectual and cultural conditioning prior to making the statement. They are both *statements of faith*, one positive, the other negative. We cannot *prove* that God exists, neither can we prove that he does not exist. The same applies to the resurrection of Jesus. The Gospel writers have never set out to prove that it actually happened. The narratives are set out simply and factually, and are based on oral traditions and the recollections of those who were there at the time, or who were close to the events recorded. There is nothing inherently inconsistent or contradictory *within* the different narratives. And though it is *not* possible to prove that the Resurrection *did not* happen, there are many who presume that it did not for want of better evidence. Having said that, not a *single witness* in history has come forward to provide one *single piece of credible evidence* that Jesus did not rise from the grave. There are many, however, who have testified that he *did*, and who are part of that living chain of witnesses from earliest times to the present day. For all its manifest imperfections and shortcomings, the church is a *sign* that Jesus *did* rise from the grave. For whatever reason we believe in something or not, it is usually bound up with our previous experience or understanding of the way the world is (our worldview). This would be the case with Richard Dawkins, on the one hand, and the Archbishop of Canterbury, on the other, to give two notable examples of people at either end of the spectrum.

The arguments and reconstructions put forward to *refute* the claim that Christ rose from the dead, that he vacated the tomb and was seen by his disciples, rest on *conjecture* alone. The only possible way to get around the facts as described and argue against the historicity of the story is to rewrite the story, as many have attempted to do. As it stands the story will speak for itself, if we allow it to do so. Though there are divergencies between the different resurrection accounts in the four gospels, on closer inspection of the nature of the detail, the accounts taken separately are entirely plausible. There would need to be a catastrophic breakdown in reason to argue otherwise. Among other things, the fact that the disciples accused the women of talking nonsense (or making no sense) on hearing their report of the empty tomb, contributes a certain authenticity to the whole story. Although belief in the resurrection of the dead was held by many Jews (the Sadducees being a notable exception), the disciples, themselves, *did not expect* Jesus to rise from the dead. The

143

idea that *he* should die and rise again was alien to Jewish expectations of their *Messiah*. It is this surprise element that provides a ring of truth to the story. Interestingly, the Jewish priestly authorities, though they themselves did not believe in bodily resurrection, seemed to take the possibility of Jesus rising from the dead more seriously than the disciples, and so they placed a guard at the tomb. This may have been a Roman guard or the Temple Guard, but a guard was placed at the tomb, nevertheless. When the tomb was found empty, the chief priests concocted a story that the soldiers had slept while on duty, during which time the body of Jesus had been removed by the disciples. Does it follow from what we are told about the disciples that they would have dared to do this and run the risk of being arrested themselves as Jesus was? Morison draws attention to this unlikely story that a Roman guard would have slept whilst on duty, for the punishment would have been execution. On the other hand, he observes, if it were the Temple Guard, this may have occurred, given the tedious circumstances of watching over a sealed tomb in a deserted garden, during the small hours of an April night. Moreover, he continues, there would have been no advantage (only considerable damage) to the Christian cause to invent such an explanation for the disappearance of the body of Jesus from the tomb (*Who Moved the Stone*, p. 190). The words and actions of the religious authorities clearly reveal an air of desperation about them. The writer of the Gospel of Matthew claims that this 'story' was still circulating at the time the Gospel was written some 40 years later. This would be how he came to know about it. If it was circulated by those who opposed the church, *how* and *why* did it find its way into the Gospel tradition? That is unless it were completely true. There is no way the Christians would have invented such a story; therefore, it must have originated outside of the first century church, which is exactly the nature of the story *itself.*

Whether or not one chooses to believe in the Resurrection, it has impacted those on both sides of the divide. It is such an extraordinary claim that it cannot be said to have made *no difference.* We may or may not have an opinion on the matter, but it has changed the world. We may or may not agree with those who believe it, but it has changed the course of history. Here we are not talking about a particular religion or religions in general. *Jesus was not religious*; in fact, he opposed the legalistic religion of his day and those who upheld it and imposed its oppressive yoke on the common people. Neither was Jesus *a political revolutionary*, in terms of worldly powers, as becomes clear in his response to the question about paying taxes: "Give to Caesar what is Caesar's and to God what is God's." (Matthew 22.21; Mark 12.17). This same attitude is seen in his retort to those who had gone to arrest him on that unforgettable night in the Garden of Gethsemane: "Am I leading a rebellion that you have come out with swords and clubs to capture me?" (Mark 14.48). The Beatitudes, however, *do* bring out the political dimension of his ministry, in terms of where real power lies and who will inherit what is truly worth possessing. Jesus succeeded in *polarising* those who were for him and those who were against him (always the inevitable outcome of God's mission; we only have to remember the Old Testament prophets), though his mission is essentially one of *reconciliation*. That is to reconcile God and the human race, and *this* was never more clearly expressed than in his words from the cross: "Father, forgive them." Today he continues to polarise those who are for and against him, but he has made a difference to the world. Hospitals, schools for the poor (original Sunday schools), our social consciousness, and gender equality, are all grounded in his teaching, example and vision.

Wherever we stand in relation to Jesus, the story of his rising from a cold tomb on a distant Sunday morning, two thousand years ago, has focused minds and challenged hearts. But how can this be *objectively proven*? We do know there exists a great *cloud of witnesses* to this extraordinary event. For certain, nothing less than a *personal encounter* with the risen Lord will serve as the definitive proof. This was true of James, the unbelieving brother of Jesus, and of Thomas who demanded proof on his own terms, insisting on his own criteria; and of Saul, whose declared intention was to destroy the church, and for which purpose he received support from the chief priests in Jerusalem. It is for each of us to make up our own minds. But we cannot sit on the fence. The world never has and never will sit on the fence, when it comes to this watershed event in human history. That we have to make up our own minds about Jesus, through a personal encounter with him, was true of some of the Samaritan villagers, who first heard about Jesus from the lips of one of the local women. By their own confession their belief was confirmed through meeting Jesus personally, rather than hearing about him from a third party (John 4.42).

Epilogue

William Neil, in his book, *The Life and Teaching of Jesus,* argues that "the Christian Church was not founded on the teaching of Jesus, but by men who believed that Jesus had risen from the grave" (p. 153). We may rush to qualify this statement by responding that the church was not founded by 'men who believed', but by Jesus, himself, who declared that he would do this very thing: "On this rock (Peter's declaration that Jesus was the Christ) I will build my church." (Matthew 16.18). However, the main thrust of Neil's argument points to the two-fold reason for the existence of the church today: the empty tomb and the post-resurrection appearances of Jesus to his followers.

With the passage of time, the world has adopted a cooler and more detached approach to the fears, turmoil and emotional confusion of the first-hand witnesses to the Resurrection. Notwithstanding editorial refinements to the story, the existence of the church today is *entirely the result* of that story handed down from generation to generation.

The Gospels tell us about the life and work of Jesus, and there are references to his life and deeds in secular history. There is no good reason why we should not accept that he *existed* and that he was a great teacher who taught primarily and authoritatively about the kingdom of God. The difficulty for many people is the *belief in miracles*. When faced with life and death situations, however, there are people who still hope and pray for a *miracle*, even if they are not sure about God. Did Jesus really perform miracles or is this the part of the story which we relegate to the world of fables and fairy-tales? If we cannot understand something, it is usually easier to *dismiss* it than to try and *understand* it. When we move into discussion about resurrection, the problem becomes even more difficult. Therefore, we resort to dismissing the story altogether. If asked to believe that Jesus rose from the dead, we might choose to believe that he did not exist in the first place, rather than try to grapple with the supernatural.

If there was only one version of the Gospel narrative, which had been written in such a way as to contradict itself in matters of substance, we would naturally suspect that it was not true, either in part or in its entirety. However, there are four gospel writers telling us about the same events from their own different perspectives. The fact that they recall the same event but in different ways is only natural, if we think about it, and is an invitation to enter into the outlook and personalities of the writers, as well as the story itself. This does not mean that where there are different details, a different ordering of events and a different set of priorities that these are to be reckoned as necessarily unhistorical. The Gospel writers each write from their own recollections of the events they describe, or from earlier written sources, oral traditions, or eyewitness testimony. Each is distinctive in its own way, and has its own particular target audience. But there is *one reason only* why the Gospels *were* written: that is the extraordinary fact of the Resurrection itself. The Gospels have come down to us not in any *uniform* way, but in *unison*. Although we refer to the four Gospels, there is, in fact, *only one*. And the message, though incredible, is clear and unequivocal.

Over two millennia, the embodiment of this gospel, the church, has made mistakes, taken wrong turnings, and developed from a popular movement into a top-heavy institution. But for all its shortcomings, it has survived, and it has also paid the price for doing so. Tertullian, a third century Church Father, from the North African city of Carthage, claimed that "the blood of the martyrs is the seed of the church," in his *Apology*, Chapter 50.13. This illuminating statement enables us to understand *how* the church has survived and prospered in the face of countless attempts to extinguish it; but *why* has it done so?

The answer to this question is firmly rooted in the purpose of Jesus to *build* his church, against which no opposition, secular or spiritual, will be able to prevail against it. But there is *more* to it than even this. Despite suffering persecution to the severest degree (sometimes organised by the state, and sometimes localised and spontaneous), the Christian faith, together with the community that embraces it, has survived and continues to grow today. Honestly, there is no *rational* answer to the question 'Why?' But there is something *super-rational* behind it. And it can *only* be this: the now faint and distant voice in a Jerusalem garden, of one *mistaken for the gardener*, really had been *heard*, and the one who spoke really had been *seen alive again*!

Postscript

Angels, Miracles and Literary Embellishments.

These three areas of discussion have generated considerable polemic in relation to the resurrection appearances of Jesus. The first two have had their existence questioned, while the third has been used to question the historical reliability of the Gospel traditions. So here follows an explanatory paragraph dealing with each in turn:

Angels are created beings. They are essentially messengers from which the name takes its meaning. They are sometimes portrayed as supernatural beings, but not always. They first feature in the Book of Genesis in connection with Abraham and his wife Sarah and also in the city of Sodom, where their striking appearance draws the attention of depraved individuals. They are *seldom* described as having wings, except in the book of the prophet Isaiah, Chapter 6, in connection with the vision in the Temple. Otherwise they often have the appearance of human beings. Billy Graham tells a story from China of angels protecting a mission compound against surrounding bandits. The next morning, the scene was described by neighbouring families who had seen four people on the roof, three sitting and one standing, quietly watching the whole night long. Angelic beings do not always fit the more exotic descriptions, but neither do excessive popular images warrant the negation of the presence and protection of angels in times of human crisis.

Miracles do not necessarily defy the laws of nature. They happen today when something good occurs for no understandable reason, often in the field of medicine. It may be possible to control such phenomena and harness the laws of nature in ways that we do not fully understand. This could apply to the miracles of Jesus. It is also worth noting that Jesus did not perform miracles for their own sake, but *for reasons of compassion and in demonstration of God's power*. They were never used in a theatrical way to draw attention to his person, although this was the inevitable result. In order to know the interaction between nature and miracles we need to understand the workings of nature more fully than at present. Miracles are often described as acts of providence or divine intervention in human affairs. In these cases, though exceptional, there would be no apparent conflict with the known laws of nature.

Embellishments of ancient texts for dramatic or other desired effect cannot be ignored by textual critics. However, it is difficult to see why such a practice would be used, if it were to undermine the acceptance or authenticity of these texts. Variants occur due to *unintentional* copyist errors. It is also widely accepted that the *most difficult* variant of a particular text is likely to be the *most authentic*. It would be reasonable for a copyist to bring greater clarity to a text or remove an apparent ambiguity, but nothing more. It would not be part of their professional remit to alter the meaning or substance of texts when their primary task is to faithfully copy the text. Extant documents from the ancient world are invariably copies of the originals. The originals have been lost and so what remains are copies of copies of the originals, and this includes the works of renowned secular writers as well as biblical texts. Subsequent readers and students of a text may also have made copies and effected *intentional* changes in order to harmonise a text and accommodate it to their own purposes. With regard to the Gospels, however, we are here contemplating *shades of meaning* rather than matters of historical substance.

Publications referred to in this book

Beasley-Murray, G. R. *The Resurrection of Jesus Christ.* Oliphants. London. 1964.

Bruce, F. F. *The New Testament Documents.* IVP. London. 1960.

Catchpole, D. *Resurrection People.* DLT. London. 2000.

Cullmann, O. *Christ and Time.* SCM. 1951.

Denney, J. *The Death of Christ.* Tyndale Press. 1951.

Hunter, A. M. *The Gospel According to St Paul.* SCM. London. 1966.

Josephus, F. Jewish Antiquities. c. AD 93 (internet extract).

McDowell, J. *Evidence that Demands a Verdict.* Paternoster. Carlisle. 1998.

Mitchell, E. The Sequence of Christ's Post-Resurrection Appearances. Online article in: 'Answers in Genesis'. 21 March, 2012.

Morison, F. *Who Moved the Stone?* Faber. 1958.

Publications referred to in this book

Morris, L. *The First Epistle of Paul to the Corinthians*. Tyndale Press. London. 1958.

Morris, L. *Studies in the Fourth Gospel*. The Paternoster Press. Exeter. 1969.

Neil, W. *The Life and Teaching of Jesus*. Hodder and Stoughton. London. 1965.

Ramsey, A. M. *The Resurrection of Jesus Christ*. Geoffrey Bles. London. 1946.

Roberts, A. et al. 'Irenæus against Heresies'. In: *The Apostolic Fathers with Justin Martyr and Irenaeus*, ed. Alexander Roberts, James Donaldson, and A. Cleveland Coxe, vol. 1, The Ante-Nicene Fathers (Buffalo, NY: Christian Literature Company, 1885).

Stevenson, J. (ed.). *A New Eusebius*. SPCK London. 1957.

Strobel, L. *The Case for Christ*. Zondervan Grand Rapids. 1998.

Tacitus, G. C. *The Annals*. AD 14-68 (internet extracts).

Tasker, R.V.G. *The Gospel According to St. John*. Tyndale Press. London. 1960.

Tenney, M. C. *New Testament Times*. Inter-Varsity Fellowship. London. 1965.

Publications referred to in this book

Tertullian, Q. S. F. *Apologeticus pro Christianis*. c. AD 197 (internet extract).

Vischer, W. 'Everywhere the Scripture is About Christ Alone'. In: *The Old Testament and Christian Faith*. Ed. Bernhard W. Anderson. SCM. London. 1964.

Williams, R. *Resurrection*: Interpreting the Easter Gospel. DLT. London. 2002.

Wright, N. T. *Surprised by Hope*. SPCK. London. 2007.

Printed in Poland
by Amazon Fulfillment
Poland Sp. z o.o., Wrocław

49877769R00092